Visits to Remarkable Places, Volume I

William Howitt

BIBLIOLIFE

Copyright © BiblioLife, LLC

BiblioLife Reproduction Series: Our goal at BiblioLife is to help readers, educators and researchers by bringing back in print hard-to-find original publications at a reasonable price and, at the same time, preserve the legacy of literary history. The following book represents an authentic reproduction of the text as printed by the original publisher and may contain prior copyright references. While we have attempted to accurately maintain the integrity of the original work(s), from time to time there are problems with the original book scan that may result in minor errors in the reproduction, including imperfections such as missing and blurred pages, poor pictures, markings and other reproduction issues beyond our control. Because this work is culturally important, we have made it available as a part of our commitment to protecting, preserving and promoting the world's literature.

All of our books are in the "public domain" and some are derived from Open Source projects dedicated to digitizing historic literature. We believe that when we undertake the difficult task of re-creating them as attractive, readable and affordable books, we further the mutual goal of sharing these works with a larger audience. A portion of BiblioLife profits go back to Open Source projects in the form of a donation to the groups that do this important work around the world. If you would like to make a donation to these worthy Open Source projects, or would just like to get more information about these important initiatives, please visit www.bibliolife.com/opensource.

VISITS

TO

REMARKABLE PLACES:

Old Halls, Battle Fields,

AND

SCENES ILLUSTRATIVE OF STRIKING PASSAGES

IN ENGLISH HISTORY AND POETRY.

BY WILLIAM HOWITT,

AUTHOR OF "THE RURAL LIFE OF ENGLAND," ETC.

IN TWO VOLUMES.

VOL. I.

PHILADELPHIA:

CAREY AND HART.

1841.

ADVERTISEMENT.

There is a passage in De Lamartine's Pilgrimage to the Holy Land, which expresses very clearly the nature and object of this work. " I have always loved to wander over the physical scenes inhabited by men I have known, admired, loved, or revered, as well amongst the living as the dead. The country which a great man has inhabited and 'preferred, during his passage on the earth, has always appeared to me the surest and most speaking relic of himself: a kind of material manifestation of his genius—a mute revelation of a portion of his soul—a living and sensible commentary on his life, actions, and thoughts. When young, I passed many solitary and contemplative hours, reclined under olive trees which shade the gardens of Horace, in sight of the delightful cascades of the Tiber; and often have I dropped to sleep in the evening, lulled by the noise of the beautiful sea of Naples, under the hanging branches of the vines, near the spot where Virgil wished his ashes to repose, because it was the most delicious site his eyes had ever beheld. How often, at a later period, have I passed mornings and evenings seated at the foot of the beautiful chestnut trees in the little valley of Charmettes, to which the remembrance of Jean Jaques Rousseau attracted me, and where I was retained by sympathy with his impressions, his reveries, his misfortunes, and his genius. And I have been thus attracted with respect to several other authors and great men, whose names and writings were deeply engraven on my memory. I wished to study them; to become acquainted with them on the spot that had given them birth, or that had inspired them; and almost always a scrutinizing glance might discover a secret and profound analogy between the country and the individual who had graced it; between the scene and the actor; between nature and the genius which derived its inspirations therefrom."

These were exactly my feelings and ideas long before De Lamartine had thus penned them down; and who, indeed, has not experienced, more or less, the same impressions? We need not visit the distant East to make the discovery; there is no country where the soil is more thickly sown with noble memories than our own, and those of the deeds, the sufferings, and the triumphs of our own progenitors. It has long been my opinion that to visit the most remarkable scenes of old English history and manners, and to record the impressions thence derived in their immediate vividness; to restore, as it were, each place and its inhabitants to freshness, and to present them freed from the dust of ages and heaviness of antiquarian rubbish piled upon them, would be a labour responded to with emphasis by readers of the present day. The general approval of the experiment made in " The Rural Life," by introducing visits to Newstead, Annesley, and Hardwicke, and the intimations of great interest in the announcement of this work, received from all quarters, convinced me that I was not mistaken.

1*

The field is a wide and a rich one. The present volumes may be considered but as precursors of others on this subject, in which I have long been engaged; and the plan of which will shortly be announced.

I have to present my warmest acknowledgments, not only to many private individuals for valuable hints and information, but also to the possessors of places visited, for the very cordial and liberal manner in which they endeavoured to promote my object.

W. H.

Esher, Dec. 18th, 1839

CONTENTS OF VOL. I.

VISIT TO PENSHURST IN KENT,

THE ANCIENT SEAT OF THE SIDNEYS.

> *   *   *   *   Tread,
> As with a pilgrim's reverential thoughts,
> The groves of Penshurst. Sidney here was born,—
> Sidney, than whom no gentler, braver man
> His own delightful genius ever feigned.
>
> SOUTHEY.

ENGLAND, amongst her titled families, can point to none more illustrious than that of Sidney. It is a name which carries with it the attestation of its genuine nobility. Others are of older standing in the realm. It is not one of those to be found on the roll of Battle Abbey. The first who bore it in England is said to have come hither in the reign of Henry III. There are others, too, which have mounted much higher in the scale of mere rank; but it may be safely said that there is none of a truer dignity, nor more endeared to the spirits of Englishmen. In point of standing and alliance, there is hardly one of our old and most celebrated

families with which it will not be found to be connected. Warwick, Leicester, Essex, Northumberland, Pembroke, Carlisle, Burleigh, Sutherland, Rutland, Strangford, Sunderland, are some of the
families united by blood or marriage with the house
and fortunes of the Sidneys. The royal blood of
England runs in the veins of their children. But it
is by a far higher nobility than that of ancient descent, or martial or political power, that the name
of Sidney arrests the admiration of Englishmen.
It is one of our great watch-words of liberty. It is
one of the household words of English veneration.
It is a name hallowed by some of our proudest historical and literary associations; identified in the
very staple of our minds with a sense of high principle, magnanimity of sentiment, and generous and
heroic devotion to the cause of our country and of
man. When we would express in a few magical
syllables all that we feel and comprehend of patriot-
ism and genius, the names that rush involuntarily to
our lips are those of Milton, Hampden, Sidney, and
such men. It is a glorious distinction for one family
to have given one such name to its country: but it
is the happiness of the house of Sidney to number
more than one such in its line, and to have enriched
our literature with a brilliant constellation of names,
both male and female, that have been themselves

poets, or the admired theme of poets; literary, or the friends of all the literary and learned of their times. They were not merely of the aristocracy of rank, but of the aristocracy of mind; and it is from that cause, and that alone, that their name is embedded like a jewel in the golden frame-work of the language.

Of this distinguished line, the most illustrious and popular was unquestionably Sir Philip. The universal admiration that he won from his cotemporaries is one of the most curious circumstances of the history of those times. The generous and affectionate enthusiasm with which he inspired both his own countrymen and foreigners, has, perhaps, no parallel. The "admirable Crichton" is the only person who occurs to our minds as presenting any thing like the same universality of knowledge and accomplishments; but Crichton was a meteor which blazed for a moment, and left only a name of wonder. Sir Philip still continues to be spoken of by all genuine poets and minds of high intellect with much of the same affectionate honour that he received from his own age. "He approaches," says Dr. Aikin, "more nearly to the idea of a perfect man, as well as of a perfect knight, than any character of any age or nation."*

* Annual Review, p. 919.

This perfection of character is shown by these
particulars: that from his boyhood he was eager for
the acquisition of all possible knowledge,—language,
philosophy, poetry, every species of art and science,
were devoured by him; yet he did not give himself
up merely to the pursuit of knowledge: he never became a mere book-worm. He was equally fond of
field sports and manly exercises. He was looked up
to as the perfect model of a courtier, without the
courtier's baseness of adulation. Elizabeth pronounced him the brightest jewel of her crown. He
was deemed the very mirror of knighthood. In the
camp he was the ardent warrior: he was sent on
foreign embassage of high importance, and proved
himself a dexterous politician. There was a universality of talent and of taste about him that marked
him as a most extraordinary man. His facility of
amassing information and putting on accomplish-
ment was marvellous. Yet he never seemed to have
any mere worldly ambition. It was the pure love
of glory that animated him; and in striving for it,
he never for a moment appeared capable of the common jealousies of emulation; on the contrary, he
was the friend, and the warm and beloved friend of
every one who was himself most distinguished. Sir
Fulke Greville, afterwards Lord Brooke, had it inscribed on his monument, as his peculiar glory, that

he was THE FRIEND OF SIR PHILIP SIDNEY. He
was the friend of Spenser, Dyer, Raleigh, Ben Jonson, Sir Henry and Sir Edward Wotton, the learned Hurbert Languet, and indeed of all the finest
spirits of his age; yet it was, after all, less by the
brilliancy of his intellect than by the warmth of his
heart, that he won so singularly on the admiration
of all men. The grand secret of his unprecedented
popularity lay in the nobility of his nature. Nothing could be more delightful than the high, un-
worldly, and incorruptible character of his mind.
It was this ardent, sunny, unselfish disposition
which was so beautiful in all his family relations.
His father, Sir Henry Sidney, himself one of the
noblest characters in history, says of him, in a letter
to his second son, Robert Sidney: " Follow the advice of your most loving brother, who in loving
you is comparable with me, or exceedeth me. Imi-
tate his virtues, exercises, studies, and actions. He
is a rare ornament of his age; the very formula
that all well-disposed young gentlemen of our court
do form also their manners and life by. In truth,
I speak it without flattery of him, or myself, *he hath
the most virtues that I ever found in any man.*"

What a proud testimony from a father to a son!
But the same admirable affection constantly displayed itself towards his brother and sister. His

2*

letters to his brother Robert are full of the most
delightfully gay, yet loving and wise spirit. Writing to him while on his travels, he declared,—what
he invariably proved by his conduct,—" There is
nothing I spend so pleaseth me as that which is for
you. If ever I have ability, you will find it ; if not,
yet shall not any brother living be better beloved
than you of me."

His tender attachment to his sister, the celebrated Countess of Pembroke, is known to all the
world. It was to Wilton that he betook himself
during his temporary absence from court, on account of his difference with the insolent Earl of
Oxford, to write his Arcadia. It was to her that
he dedicated it, and more than dedicated it, calling
it " Pembroke's Arcadia." It was to her that he
sent it, sheet by sheet, when he was not present
with her to read it to her; living in her approbation
of it, and seeking no other fame from it, for it was
not published till after his death.

Such were the noble and endearing qualities that
made Sir Philip Sidney the idol of his times in
foreign countries as much as in his own ; that induced Poland to offer him its crown ; that covered
his hearse with the laments of all the learned and
poetical amongst his cotemporaries—three volumes
of such funereal tributes in various languages being

published on the occasion of his death; the two great English universities striving which should outdo the other in number and intensity of its " melodious tears."

The evidences of Sir Philip Sidney's genius which have come down to us are to be found in his Arcadia; his Astrophel and Stella; his Defence of Poesy; his Sonnets and Songs: and there have not been wanting those who assert that they do not bear out by their merit the enthusiastic encomiums of his cotemporaries. Lord Orford has pronounced the Arcadia " a tedious, lamentable, pedantic, pastoral romance;" and Hume, Tytler, and others, have echoed the opinion.

How many are there of our own age who are prepared by actual perusal to sanction or disallow of this dictum? How many have read that poem of which every one speaks as a matter of knowledge—Spenser's Faery Queen? How many, even, have waded through Paradise Lost? Every poetical spirit which has qualified itself to give an answer, must declare that the literary relics of Sir Philip Sidney,—writings thrown off rapidly in the midst of many pursuits and many distracting attentions, and before death at the early age of thirty-two,—must pronounce them well worthy of his fame.

His poetry and prose too have all the marks of stiffness, and affected point of that period ; but every page of his composition abounds with sober and with brilliant thoughts. His sonnets are delightful testimonies to the inward beauty and tenderness of the man. Many readers have been made familiar with the fine opening of one of his sonnets, by Wordsworth introducing it as the opening of one of his :—

> With how sad steps, O Moon, thou climb'st the sky,
> How silently, and with how sad a face!

and every real lover of poetry, if he opens the volume of Sir Philip Sidney, will find much that will equally delight him, and generate within him trains of high and sober thought.

But, in my opinion, it is the Arcadia which must stand as the best image of his "inner man." Whoever reads it, should read it with reference to the spirit of the age, and turn relentlessly over all the pastoral episodes, and he will then find a volume full of stirring interest, striking invention, and that living tone of high, pure, heroic spirit, which scorned every thing base; which is, in truth, the grand characteristic of Sidney;—a spirit which stands up by the low and cunning knowingness of our own day, like one of the statues of Greece by the wigged and sworded objects of modern sculpture.

Such passages as the Prayer of Pamela are amongst the noblest specimens of impassioned eloquence in the language. Charles I. showed how deeply that passage had touched him by adopting it as his own petition to the Supreme Being as he went to the scaffold; and the closing portion of it shall close these passing remarks on Sir Philip Sidney's writings, as very expressive of his nature. —" Let calamity bee the exercise, but not the overthrow of my virtue. Let the power of my enemies prevail, but prevail not to my destruction. Let my greatness bee their prey, let my pain bee the sweetness of their revenge; let them, if so it seems good unto thee, vex me with more and more punishment: but, O Lord, let never their wickedness have such a hand, but that I may carry a pure mind in a pure body!"

The death of Sir Philip Sidney, from a wound received on the field of Zutphen, has become celebrated by the circumstance continually referred to as an example of the most heroic magnanimity— giving up the water for which he had earnestly implored to a dying soldier near—saying, " he has more need of it than I." But the whole of his behaviour from that time to the hour of his death,

twenty-five days afterwards, was equally characteristic,—being spent amongst his friends in the
exercise of the most exemplary patience and sweetness of temper, and in the discussion of such solemn
topics as the near view of eternity naturally brings
before the spirit of the dying Christian.

Algernon Sidney is as fine a character, though
seen under another and a sterner aspect. He was
born to more troublous times and a less courtly
scene. He had evidently formed himself upon a
model of Roman virtue. He was a pure republican,
placing public virtue before him as his guide, from
which neither interest nor ambition were ever able
to make him swerve ; and that such was his life as
well as his creed, has been nobly avowed by a
great writer of very opposite political profession.

> Great men have been amongst us; hands that penned
> And tongues that uttered wisdom, better none ;
> The later Sidney, Marvel, Harrington,
> Young Vane, and others who called Milton friend.
> These moralists could act and comprehend ;
> They knew how genuine glory is put on ;
> Taught us how rightfully a nation shone
> In splendour ; what strength was that would not bend
> But in magnanimous weakness.
>
>   WORDSWORTH.

We see in his portraits the firm and melancholy

look of a man who had grown up for political martyrdom, and the times afforded him but too much opportunity to arrive at it. The words of one of his letters to his father, Lord Leicester,* are more demonstrative of his character than the most laboured exposition of it by any other man can be. —"I walk in the light God hath given me : if it be dimme or uncertaine I must beare the penalty of my errors. I hope to do it with patience, and that noe burthen should be very grevious to me except sinne and shame! God keepe me from these evils, and in all things else dispose of me according to his pleasure." They were singular coincidences, that these two great men of one family died young— one in the field and the other on the scaffold; and that each had a sister celebrated for their charms by the poets, and one herself a poet—the Countess of Pembroke, "Sidney's sister, Pembroke's mother;" and Waller's Saccharissa.

In thus noticing the exalted principles and splen-did characters of these Sidneys, it is a very natural and important question, what were the influences under which such men and women sprung up from one stock? Ben Jonson, in his visit to Robert Sidney, Sir Philip's brother, when Earl of Leicester, can partly let us into the secret :

* Blencowe's Sidney Papers.

They are and have been taught religion.   Thence
Their gentle spirits have sucked innocence.
Each morne and even they are taught to pray
With the whole household, and may every day
Reade in their virtuous parents' noble parts,
The mysteries of manners, arms, and arts.

The Forest, ii.

Sir Philip Sidney grew under the most favour-
able auspices.   His mother was Mary Dudley, the
daughter of the Duke of Northumberland, and sister
of Lord Guildford Dudley, the husband of Lady
Jane Grey.   The tragedies which the enthronement
of Lady Jane brought into her family, made her
retire from the world, and devote herself to the
careful education of her children.   His father, Sir
Henry Sidney, was, as I have already observed,
one of the noblest and best of men, and one who,
had he not been eclipsed by the glory of his descendants, must have occupied more of the attention
of the English historian than he has done.   In his
arms expired the pious young prince, Edward VI.,
who entertained the warmest friendship for him;
and his conduct in the government of Ireland, of
which he was thrice Lord Deputy, and all his
recorded sentiments, exhibit him a rare example of
integrity and wisdom.

Such were some of the Sidneys of other days;

and, as if poetry were destined to break forth with periodical lustre in this family, it has now to add Percy Bysshe Shelley to its enduring names; for Shelley was a lineal Sidney. The present Sir John Shelley Sidney being his paternal uncle, and his cousin Philip Sidney, Lord de L'Isle, being the present possessor of Penshurst.

In these preliminary pages I have traced some of the causes which must throw a lasting and peculiar interest around Penshurst; let us now hasten thither at once.

Having received from Lord de L'Isle an order to see every thing of public interest at Penshurst, accompanied by an expectation that he would himself be there, and ready to give me all the information in his power, I went there on Tuesday, September 25th, 1838.

I took coach to Tunbridge on Monday, and after breakfast on Tuesday morning walked on to Penshurst through a delightful country; now winding along quiet green lanes, and now looking out on the great beautiful dale in which Tunbridge stands, and over other valleys to my left. Green fields and rustic cottages interspersed amongst woods; and

the picturesque hop-grounds on the steep slopes and
in the hollows of the hills, now in their full glory;
and all the rural population out and busy in gathering the hops, completed such scenery as I expected
to find in the lovely county of Kent.

The whole road as I came from town was
thronged with huge wagons of pockets of new hops,
piled nearly as high as the houses they passed, a
great quantity of these going up out of Sussex; and
here, at almost every farm-house and group of
cottages, you perceived the rich aromatic odour of
hops, and saw the smoke issuing from the cowls of
the drying kilns. The whole county was odorifer-
ous of hop.

The first view which I got of the old house of
Penshurst, called formerly both Penshurst Place and
Penshurst Castle,* was as I descended the hill
opposite to it. Its gray walls and turrets, and high-
peaked and red roofs rising in the midst of them;
and the new buildings of fresh stone, mingled with
the ancient fabric, presented a very striking and
venerable aspect.

It stands in the midst of a wide valley, on a
pleasant elevation; its woods and park strecthing
away beyond, northwards; and the picturesque

* Originally Pencester.

church, parsonage, and other houses of the village, grouping in front.

From whichever side you view the house, it strikes you as a fitting abode of the noble Sidneys. Valleys run out on every side from the main one in which it stands; and the hills, which are everywhere at some distance, wind about in a very pleasant and picturesque manner, covered with mingled woods and fields, and hop-grounds. The park ranges northward from the house in a gently-ascending slope, and presents you with many objects of interest, not merely in trees of enormous growth, but in trees to which past events and characters have given an everlasting attraction; especially Sir Philip Sidney's Oak, Saccharissa's Walk, and Gamage's Bower. Southey and Waller have both celebrated the Sidney oak. Southey says,—

> That stately oak,
> Itself hath mouldered now:

Zouch, in his life of Sir Philip, on the contrary, says it was cut down in 1768. It is probable that both statements are erroneous; for the oak which tradition has called " the Sidney Oak," and " the Bear's Oak," no doubt in allusion to the Bear-and-ragged-staff in the Leicester arms, is still standing

Probably the one cut down, was what Ben Jonson calls " the Ladies' Oak."

Amongst the many tributes of respect to Penshurst, none are so graphic and complete as that of Ben Jonson.   This is to the life.   You see in every line that the stout old dramatist had walked over the ground, and beheld the house and the people he describes.   We shall have speedy reason to recur to this description to show how true to the fact it is.

> Thou art not, Penshurst, built to envious show
> Of touch, or marble ; nor canst boast a row
> Of polished pillars, or a roofe of gold :
> Thou hast no lantherne whereof tales are told ;
> Or stayre, or courts; but standst an ancient pile,
> And these grudged at, art reverenced the while.
> Thou joyst in better markes, of soyle, of ayre,
> Of wood, of water : therein 'thou are faire.
> Thou hast thy walks for health as well as sport ;
> Thy Mount to which the Dryads do resort,
> Where Pan and Bacchus their high feasts have made,
> Beneath the broad beech and the chestnut shade.
> That taller tree, which of a nut was set
> At his great birth where all the Muses met.
> There, in the writhed bark are cut the names
> Of many a sylvane token with his flames.
> And thence the ruddy Satyres oft provoke
> The lighter Fawnes to reach thy Ladies's Oake.
>   Thy coppe, too, named of Gamage, thou hast there,
> That never fails to serve thee seasoned deere,

When thou wouldst feast, or exercise thy friends.
The lower land, that to the river bends,
Thy sheepe, thy bullocks, kine and calves do feed ;
The middle ground thy mares and horses breed.
Each banke doth yield thee coneys ; and the topps,
Fertile of wood, Ashore and Sidney's copps,
To crowne thy open table doth provide
The purpled pheasant with the speckled side ;
Thy painted partrich lyes in every field,
And for thy messe is willing to be killed ;
And if the high-swoln Medway faile thy dish,
Thou hast thy ponds that pay thee tribute fish ;
Fat, aged carpe, that runne into thy net,
And pikes, now weary their owne kinde to eat,
As loth the second draught, or cast to stay,
Officiously, at first, themselves betray.
Bright eels that emulate them, leape on land
Before the fisher, or into his hand.

   Thou hast thy orchard fruit, thy garden flowers,
Fresh as the ayre, and new as are the hours.
The early cherry with the later plum,
Fig, grape, and quince, each in his time doth come.
The blushing apricot and woolly peach
Hang on thy walls that every child may reach.
And though thy walls be of the country stone,
They're reared with no man's ruin, no man's grone.
There's none that dwell about them wish them downe ;
But all come in, the farmer and the clowne,
And no one empty-handed, to salute
Thy lord and lady though they have no suite.
Some bring a capon, some a rural cake,

Some nuts, some apples; some that think they make
The better cheeses, bring 'hem; or else send
By their ripe daughters, whom they would commend
This way to husbands; and whose baskets beare
An emblem of themselves in plum or peare.

But what can this (more than express their love)
Adde to thy free provisions, far above
The need of such! whose liberal boord doth flow
With all that hospitalitie doth know!
Where comes no guest but is allowed to eate
Without his feare, and of thy lord's owne meate;
Where the same beere, and breade, and self-same wine
That is his lordship's shall be also mine.
And I not faine to sit (as some this day
At great men's tables) and yet dine away.
Here no man tells my cups; nor standing by,
A waiter doth my gluttony envy:
But gives me what I call, and lets me eate;
He knows below, he shall find plentie of meate.
Thy tables hoard not up for the nexte day,
Nor when I take my lodging need I pray
For fire, or lights, or livorie; all is there,
As if thou, then, wert mine, or I reigned here.
There's nothing I can wish, for which I stay.
This found King James when hunting late this way,
With his brave sonne the prince; they saw thy fires
Shine bright on every hearth, as the desires
Of thy Penates had been set on flame
To entertaine them, or the country came
With all their zeale to warme their welcome here.
What great (I will not saye but) sodayne cheare

Didst thou then make 'hem! and what praise was heaped
On thy good lady then! who, therein, reaped
The just reward of her high houswifry;
To have her linen, plate, and all things nigh
When she was farre; and not a room but drest
As if it had expected such a guest!

These, Penshurst, are thy praise; and yet not all.
Thy lady's noble, fruitfull, chaste withall.
His children, thy great lord may call his owne;
A fortune in this age but rarely knowne.
They are and have been taught religion; thence
Their gentler spirits have sucked innocence.
Each morn and even they are taught to pray,
With the whole household, and may, every day,
Reade, in their vertuous parents' noble parts
The mysteries of manners, arms, and arts.

Now, Penshurst, they that will proportion thee
With other edifices, when they see
Those proud, ambitious heaps, and nothing else,
May say, their lords have built, but thy lord dwells.

BEN JONSON.—*The Forrest*, ii.

The house now presents two principal fronts.
The one facing westward, formerly looked into a
court, called the President's Court, because the
greater part of it was built by Henry Sidney, the
father of Sir Philip, and Lord President of the
Council established in the Marches of Wales. The
court is now thrown open, and converted into a
lawn surrounded by a sunk fence, and overlooking

a quiet valley of perhaps a mile in length, terminated by woody hills of great rural beauty. This
court will eventually be laid out in a flower garden; Lord de L'Isle having fitted up the suite of
rooms in this, and the north front, for the family
use, including dining and drawing rooms, library,
and other rooms, which have been done under the
superintendence of Mr. Rebecca, of Piccadilly, in
the very best taste; exhibiting, at once, a striking
unity with the general character of the old pile, and
yet possessing all the elegance and convenience
required by modern habits. Oak wainscoting has
been introduced, yet not in such heaviness and
profusion as to take away from that sense of finish
and of comfort that we now look for in a place of
family abode; and the ceilings, with their cornices
and compartments, partake of the same character.
They display true keeping and good sense. You
meet with none of that extravagance and broken-
up-ness of design which offend you in many attempts to restore the ancient mansion, and to adapt
it to present uses. You do not, as you advance,
find yourself at this moment in a Chinese room, in
the next in an Egyptian, and then in an Italian or
a French one. All is English, and English of the
right date, which is rarer still. The ornaments are
taken from the family arms; and while they con-

tinually remind you that you are in the abode of
the Sidneys and the Leicesters, you are also reminded by the freshness of all the finishings, that
you are there too in the days of their polished
descendants.

This front, as well as the northern one, is of
great length. It is of several dates and styles of
architecture. The façade is of two stories, and
battlemented. The centre division, which is of
recent erection, has large windows of triple arches,
with armonial shields between the upper and lower
stories. The south end of the façade is of an ancient date, with smaller mullioned windows; the
northern portion with windows of a similar character to those in the centre, but less and plainer.
Over this façade shows itself the tall gable of the
ancient banqueting hall which stands in the inner
court. At each end of the façade projects a wing,
with its various towers of various bulk and height;
some square, of stone, others octagon, of brick,
with a great diversity of tall, worked chimneys,
which, with steep roofs, and the mixture of brick-
work and stone-work all through the front, give a
mottled, but yet very venerable aspect to it.

The north and principal front, facing up the
park, has been restored by its noble possessor, and
presents a battlemented range of stone buildings of

various projections, towers, turrets, and turreted chimneys, which, when the windows are put in, which is not yet fully done, will have few superiors amongst the castellated mansions of England.

The old gateway tower remains, and still forms the carriage entrance. On its front was fixed aloft, a hatchment quartering the royal arms with those of the Sidneys, denoting the death of Lady de L'Isle, the daughter of the late king. Over the door is a stone tablet with this inscription:—

THE MOST RELIGIOUS AND RENOWNED PRINCE EDWARD THE SIXTH KINGE OF ENGLAND FRANCE AND IRELAND GAVE THIS HOUSE OF PENCESTER WITH THE MANNORS LANDES AND APPURTENANCES THER UNTO BELONGINGE UNTO HIS TRUSTYE AND WEL-BELOVED SERVANT SYR WILLIAM SYDNY KNIGHT BANNARET SERVINGE HIM FROM THE TYME OF HIS BIRTH UNTO HIS CORONATION IN THE OFFICES OF CHAMBERLAYNE AND STUARDE OF HIS HOUSEHOLD IN COMMEMORATION OF WHICH MOST WORTHIE AND FAMOUS KINGE SIR HENRIE SYDNEY KNIGHT OF THE MOST NOBLE ORDER OF THE GARTER LORD PRESIDENT OF THE COUNCIL ESTABLISHED IN THE MARCHES OF WALES SONNE AND HEYRE OF THE AFORE NAMED SYR WILLIAM CAUSED THIS TOWER TO BE BUYLDED AND THAT MOST EXCELLENT PRINCES ARMS TO BE ERECTED ANNO DOMINO 1585.

The royal arms are accordingly emblazoned in stone on another tablet beneath.

Immediately on the right hand of this gateway, as you front it, remains a piece of ancient brick front with its armorial escutcheons, tall octagon brick tower, and cross-banded chimneys. The rest, with the exception of the stone tower terminating the western end, is all new; containing another entrance arch, with the family arms emblazoned above it, and which, with its Elizabethan windows, corbels, and shields, is in excellent keeping with the old portion.

From the eastern end of this front runs a fine avenue of limes, and at a short distance in the park is Gamage's Bower, now a mere woody copse, as represented by Ben Jonson.

In the centre of the inner court stands the old Banqueting Hall, a tall gabled building with high red roof, surmounted with the ruins of a cupola, erected upon it by Mr. Perry, who married the heiress of the family, but who does not seem to have brought much taste into it. On the point of each gable is an old stone figure—the one a tortoise, the other a lion couchant;—and upon the back of each of these old figures, so completely accordant with the building itself, which exhibits under its eaves and at the corners of its windows

numbers of these grotesque corbels which distin-
guish our buildings of an early date, both domestic
and ecclesiastical, good Mr. Perry clapped a huge
leaden vase which had probably crowned aforetime
the pillars of a gateway, or the roof of a garden-
house.   It is to be hoped that Lord de L'Isle will
not long delay his intention of having these mon-
strosities pitched from their undeserved elevation.*

With these exceptions, this hall, of which I shall
have more to say anon, bears externally every
mark of a very ancient building.

The south side of the house has all the irregu-
larity of an old castle, consisting of various towers,
projections, buttresses, and gables.   Some of the
windows show tracery of a superior order, and
others have huge common sashes, introduced by
the tasteful Mr. Perry aforesaid.   The court on this
side is surrounded by battlemented walls, and has a
massy square gatehouse, leading into the old garden, or pleasaunce, which sloped away down towards the Medway, but is now merely a grassy
lawn, with the remains of one fine terrace running
along its western side.

In this court, opposite the door of the Banqueting

* Since the above was written the cupola and vases have
been removed.

Hall, hangs a large bell, on a very simple frame of wood. The whole has a genuine look of the ancient time when hunters came hungry from the forest, and needed no gilded belfry to summon them to dinner. On the bell is inscribed in raised letters:

ROBERT EARL OF LEICESTER, AT PENSHURST, 1649.

The old banqueting hall is a noble specimen of the baronial hall of the reign of Edward III., when both house and table exhibited the rudeness of a martial age, and both gentle and simple revelled together, parted only by the salt. The floor is of brick. The raised platform, or dais, at the west-end, advances sixteen feet into the room. The width of the hall is about forty feet, and the length of it about fifty-four feet. On each side are tall gothic windows, much of the tracery of which has been some time knocked out, and the openings plastered up. At the east-end is a fine large window, with two smaller ones above it; but the large window is, for the most part, hidden by the front of the music gallery. In the centre of the floor an octagon space is marked out with a rim of stone, and within this space stands a massy old dog, or brand-iron, about a yard and half wide, and the two upright ends three feet six inches high, having

on their outer sides, near the top, the double broad
arrow of the Sydney arms. The smoke from the
fire, which was laid on this jolly dog, ascended and
passed out through the centre of the roof, which is
high, and of framed oak, and was adorned at the
spring of the huge groined spars with grotesque
projecting carved figures, or corbels, which are
now taken down, being considered in danger of
falling, and are laid in the music gallery.

The whole of this fine old roof is, indeed, in a
very decayed state, and unless repaired and made
proof against the weather, must, ere many winters
be over, come down; a circumstance extremely to
be regretted, being said to be the oldest specimen
of our ancient banqueting hall remaining.

The massy oak tables remain. That on the dais,
or the lord's table, is six yards long, and about one
wide; and at this simple board no doubt Sir Philip
and Algernon Sidney, the Countess of Pembroke,
Saccharissa, Waller, Ben Jonson, and though last
mentioned, many a noble, and some crowned heads,
have many a time dined. What a splendid group,
indeed, may imagination summon up and set down
at this rude table, where unquestionable history will
warrant us in placing them. At one time the gentle
and pious Edward VI.; at another his more domi-
neering and shrewd sister Elizabeth, with her proud

favourite, Leicester or Essex, Cecil or Warwick, all allied to, or in habits of intimacy with, the lord of the house. James the First, and Charles, then prince, no doubt took their seats here, at that un-looked-for visit of which Ben Jonson speaks; and the paintings in the gallery, and rooms above, will show us many a high-born beauty, and celebrated noble and gentleman who have graced this old hall with their presence, and made its rafters echo to their wit and merriment.

The tables down the sides of the hall, at which the yeomen retainers and servants sate, are seven yards long, and of a construction several degrees less in remove from the common trestle.

At the lower end of the hall is a tall wainscot screen supporting the music gallery, the plainness and even rudeness of its fashion marking the earliness of its date. The space betwixt it and the end of the hall, forms a passage from one court to the other, and serves also to conceal the entrances to the kitchen, larder, and other similar offices.

Most of the wainscot and doors of this part of the house are of split oak, never touched with a plane, but reduced to their proper dimensions only by the chisel and the hatchet; sufficient proof of their antiquity. The arched passages and doorways from the courts to the hall are nevertheless of excellent style and workmanship,

At the back of the music-gallery, and up to the very top of the hall, hang shields, matchlocks with their rests, steel caps, banners, and different pieces of armour; but much the greater portion of those trophies has fallen down, and they lie in the music-gallery, or some of the disused rooms.

On each side of the dais, as in our old colleges, ascends a flight of loo stairs; one leading to the old apartments of the house, the other into a sort of little gallery, out of which the lord could look into the hall, and call his wassailers to order if any unusual clamour or riot was going on, or to call any of his retainers, bells not then being introduced.

On the right hand of the dais, is the entrance into the cellar; an odd situation to our present fancy, but then, no doubt, thought very convenient for the butler to bring up the wine to the lord's table. Passing this cellar door to the right of the dais, and ascending the loo stairs, you find yourself in the ball-room: a large room, with two ancient lustre chandeliers surmounted with the crown-royal, and said to have been the first made in England, and presented by Elizabeth to the Earl of Leicester. In this room are several columns of verde-antique, giallo, and porphyry from Italy; antique burial-urns, and old tables of mosaic marble. There are four large frescoes by Vanderbrecht:—The Triumph of Cupid; Venus rising from the Sea; Europa on the Bull; and Cupid trying his Bow. Amongst some indifferent portraits is one of Lady E. Sidney, and another of Lady Egerton.

In the pages' room are numerous paintings. Amongst them are the Duke of St. Albans, Nell Gwynn's son, a boy of about eight or ten years of age, in a rich murrey-coloured doublet and breeches, with roses at his knees and on his shoes; an excellent painting. Head of John Dudley Duke of Northumberland, 1545: the father of Lord Guildford Dudley; of the Earls of Warwick and Leicester; and of Mary Dudley, the mother of Sir Philip Sidney. Head of the Duchess of Portsmouth: small full-length of Algernon Percy Earl of Northumberland: the Egerton family, three children: head of old Parr, who died at the age of one hundred and fifty-two: Catherine Cecil, Countess of Leicester, of whom there are several other portraits in the house: head of Algernon Sidney, in a defective state: Duns Scotus: supposed portrait of General Leslie.

There is a small recumbent statue of Cleopatra

4*

from Herculaneum, here; and the bridle of the Duke of Buckingham, the favourite of James I., hangs by one of the windows. The front, martingal, and the bosses of the bits, gilt and much ornamented.

Queen Elizabeth's Room.—It is said that Elizabeth, when visiting Sir Henry Sidney, the father of Sir Philip, furnished this room. The chairs are fine, tall, and capacious ones, the frames gilded, and the drapery yellow and crimson satin, richly embroidered. They must have been very splendid when in their full glory. The walls of each end of the room are covered with similar embroidered satin, said, as in all such cases, to have been worked by the queen and her attendants.

Here stand the three most interesting portraits in the house. Those of Sir Philip, Algernon, and Mary Sidney, the Countess of Pembroke.

Sir Philip Sidney is here apparently not more than two or three and twenty years of age. His dress is a rich laced doublet of pale crimson; ruff, and scarlet mantle hanging loosely from his shoulder. He is standing reading, with a staff of office in his hand, and with his armour about him. It is a lively portrait, very much resembling that belonging to the Duke of Bedford, from which Lodge's engraving is taken; and also that in Warwick Castle; but of a younger aspect than either. It perhaps does not come up to your idea of the knightly beauty and grace of Sir Philip Sidney; for few indeed of the portraits of the great men of that wonderful era do realize your conceptions of them; but it has all the truth and light-heartedness of youth about it, and breathes of that high-minded nobility and generous enthusiasm for whatever was heroic and just, which distinguished him. You cannot look long on the high forehead, clear earnest eyes, and smooth features, without feeling that they belonged to the youthful poet, and gallant and unselfish hero. His hair is cut short behind, and turned aside from his forehead, and what is perhaps most unlooked for, its colour is of a ruddy brown. It is not red hair of the common hue, nor chestnut, but a dusky red, or ruddy brown, and which is proved by a circumstance to which I shall soon advert, to have really been the colour of Sir Philip's hair. His complexion is also that of a person who has a tinge of the red in his hair. The same tinge is visible in the hair of many of the Sidneys, both as seen in their portraits and in locks which are preserved.

Lodge's portrait of the Countess of Pembroke is a very good transcript,

Algernon Sidney is also here represented as we

see him in the engravings ;—standing by a column,
leaning on a folio book labelled LIBERTAS. He is
in a buff coat embroidered, a scarlet sash, and
steel cuirass. The tower where he was beheaded
is in view, and the axe of the executioner behind.
His long dark-brown hair is combed over his
shoulders; his nose is Roman ; and the expression
of the whole countenance stern and melancholy.
From the emblems of his fate about him, it is evident that this painting was done after his death.
The original likeness is in the gallery.

Near these is Lord Lisle, the son of Lady Egerton, by Lely: Robert Spencer, Earl of Sunderland,
the husband of Saccharissa : Col. Thomas Sidney,
his wife and child, the father and mother of Mrs.
Perry, the grandmother of Sir John Shelley Sidney.
The Earl of Leicester, 1618; Robert, Earl of Leicester, 1632, by Vandyke : Philip, Lord Lisle, Earl
of Leicester, 1678: his mother, again, Lady Elizabeth Sidney (a Bridgewater Egerton): and the present Lord de L'Isle. Robert Dudley, Queen Elizabeth's Earl of Leicester, by Gerard : Ambrose
Dudley, his brother, Earl of Warwick; Henry Rich,
Earl of Holland, by Vandyke. A large family-
piece—Barbara Gamage, Countess of Leicester,
1596, and her six children, all in the formal dress
of the time. In this room are various other family

portraits, and George III. and Queen Charlotte, by Gainsborough. There is a sleeping Venus, by Titian; a Charity, by Guido; and perhaps, as a painting, the most attractive piece of all is a Van-dyke, Philip Lord Lisle—a boy with his dog, and his hunting-pole upon his shoulder. He has on an embroidered scarf and buskins, richly worked with gold. He appears to be advancing through a wood, and his attention is arrested by something in the trees before him. The whole figure is full of youth-ful buoyancy, and the countenance of grace and nature.

Tapestry Room.—Full-lengths of William and Mary: William IV., by Sir Thomas Lawrence: Edward VI., by Holbein, an excellent portrait: Sir Henry Sidney, the president, in a black velvet cap and robe; a portrait in keeping with his character as a high-minded gentleman.

The most curious painting in this room is how-ever, perhaps, one containing the portraits of the two celebrated sisters, Lady Dorothy Percy, Coun-tess of Leicester, and Lady Lucy Percy, Countess of Carlisle. These ladies, daughters of the Duke of Northumberland, so well known in their own day, are well known too by their portraits in Lodge. Here they are given together, and the variation of their characters is obvious in their persons. The

Countess of Leicester is a woman of that bold beauty which answers to what we know of her; a woman who seemed born to command and to be admired. She had quick passions and a strong will, but she knew both her own nature, and was quick to see that of all who came about her. She had great self-command, and could fascinate, or repel by a cool air of dignity, at her pleasure. Her husband has left us, in his letters, a very touching account of her death-bed farewell of him. She was the mother of Algernon Sidney, and looking on her fine, but firm, and high-spirited face, we recognize at once the source of his lofty and unbending qualities.

The Countess of Carlisle was a woman of similar character in many points, but more devoted to political intrigue. " Lady Carlisle," says Miss Aikin in her Memoirs of the Reign of Charles I., " was a distinguished beauty, wit, and political intriguer, nor is her memory free from the suspicion, at least, of gallantry ; no court lady of her time was equally celebrated or conspicuous. She was flattered in French by Voiture, and in her native tongue by almost all the contemporary wits and poets, and more especially by Waller in verse, and in prose by that singular and mysterious person Sir Toby Matthew ; who composed an elaborate character of her, which is sufficiently hyperbolical to wear some appearance of irony, especially in the eulogium which he seems to bestow upon that arrogant scorn with which it was her practice to treat persons of every rank. . . . She was early appointed to a high office in the household of the queen; and notwithstanding occasional quarrels, such as could scarcely fail to arise between two ladies so distinguished for high spirit, she long enjoyed and singularly abused the favour and confidence of Henrietta." Wentworth is supposed at one period to have stood high in her good graces, and even Laud paid homage at her shrine.

Here are besides, heads of William and Mary: Nell Gwynn, by Lely, as a Venus lying on a couch with a child standing by her; a strange picture, but beautifully executed. Some family pictures; a sea-piece, by John Tennant, a fisherman looking out with a spying-glass: a curious old piece a music party: a head of a female, by Giorgione, full of strong character; and St. Peter delivered out of Prison, by Steenwick. There are on the walls two large pieces of Gobelin tapestry; Eolus unbarring the winds; and the triumph of Ceres. A card table stands here, given by Queen Elizabeth, the middle of which is covered with needlework, embroidery of the very kind now so much worked by our young ladies.

Picture Closet.—Algernon Percy as high-admiral of England: Titian's Mistress, by himself; a soft fattish woman with yellow hair, but beautifully painted: Madonna and sleeping Christ, by Guido; the face of the Madonna full of expression, and the light thrown upon it with fine effect: head of a Saint, by Giorgione, in a praying attitude with clasped hands, the colour of the flesh is of a rich deep yellow, as if the saint were the inhabitant of a sultry country: a Crucifixion: Bandits, by Spagnoletto; and various small pieces by good masters.

The Gallery.—A Flemish Womam, by Peter Thoue, 1560, with fruit, very good: a curious old piece, a Madonna and Child, probably brought from some ancient shrine: full-length of Lady Mary Dudley, wife of Sir Henry, and mother of Sir Philip Sidney, with a guitar, and in a rich embroidered gown of Elizabethan ruff, her hair frizzled close to her head: the original portrait of Algernon Sidney, by Verres: Languet, Sir Philip Sidney's friend: Bacchanals, by N. Poussin: piece on marble, a Woman with her Distaff, and a Shepherd playing on his pipe, with sheep and cattle about: James Stuart, Duke of Richmond, by Vandyke: Dying Mother, probably copied from Murillo: Abraham offering up Isaac, a large piece, by Guercino da Cento: a Procession, by Rubens, evidently a piece full of life and grace from what little can be seen of the figures, but nearly invisible from want of cleaning: Telemachus in the island of Calypso.

Dorothea, Countess of Sunderland, by Hoskins, that is, Saccharissa after her marriage: on the other side of the gallery is Saccharissa before her marriage—Dorothea Sidney, by Vandyke. She is represented as a shepherdess in a straw hat, the brim of which is lined with blue satin, her hair is disposed in ringlets on each side of the face, leaving the crown of the head smooth and round in the favourite fashion of the time. Like that of the Sidneys in general, it has a ruddy, or in her case, rather golden tinge. For beauty, the portrait of Hoskins, done after her marriage, has the highest claim; but though there is great softness of figure and complexion about this lady, we are led by the praises of Waller, to look for more striking charms than we immediately perceive in Saccharissa. As in Sir Philip Sidney, so in this celebrated female of his race, there were undoubtedly those fascinations of manner and spirit, which, though visible to all beholders, have escaped the hand of the painter.

Virgin, Child, and St. John, said to be a copy from Rafaelle, but admirably painted. Joseph's wrinkled face, full of admiring devotion, and the brunette beauty of Mary, are equally excellent; the dark eye and rich lips of the Madonna, are full of maternal satisfaction, and deep holy joy: Maleager and Atalanta, a large piece, indistinct from want of cleaning: the scourging of Christ, by Spagnoletto, the same: Holy Family, by Bassano, the same: a boy's head, by Caracci: Christ crowned with thorns, a large piece, of great merit, but artist not named: a very large family-piece of the Perrys, including the wife of Bysshe Shelley, and mother of Sir John Shelley Sidney: head of Thomas, Earl of Surrey: Ann Percy, Lady Stanhope, by Nestcher: Bacchanals, by N. Poussin: Endymion, by Bartolomeo: a modern country coquette, by Wyatt: Abbot, Archbishop of Canterbury, a curious old piece: Thomas Wentworth, constable of Queenborough Castle in the first of Richard III.: a drunken gondolier, by Rubens: Apollo and the Muses, after Vandyke. In this part of the gallery stands an ebony cabinet, with small brass figures in little niches and paintings on the panels, which was given by James I. to the first Earl of Leicester.

Head of William Paulet, Marquis of Winchester,

a very old man: Sir William Sidney, to whom Penshurst was given by Edward VI., by Lucas de Héer: Madonna and Christ, by Andrea del Sarto. The most curious piece in the gallery, and indeed in the house, is one of Sir Philip Sidney, and his brother Robert, afterwards first Earl of Leicester of this line. Sir Philip, a youth of perhaps sixteen, is standing arm in arm with Robert, a boy of about thirteen or fourteen. They are in a court dress, both exactly alike, a sort of doublet and collar. The collar is just the boy's collar of the present day, except that it is fringed with lace. The doublet is buttoned down the front with close set buttons, it is fitted exactly to the body with very close sleeves, and turned up with lace cuffs. The colour of the doublet is French gray. They have trunk-hose, very full indeed, of crimson figured satin, stockings and garters of the same colour as the doublet, with roses at the knees, and on the shoes. Their shoes are of leather, with tan-coloured soles, and are cut high in the instep; having much the look of listing shoes of the present day: their swords complete their costume. Their hair is cut short behind and turned aside on the forehead. There is a hat of white beaver lying on a table close to the elbow of Sir Philip, with a stiff upright plume of ostrich feathers with edges dyed crimson.

The lads have a strong likeness as brothers, and bear the same likeness to the portrait of Sir Philip in Queen Elizabeth's room. Philip has something of an elder-brother, patronizing air, and is full of a frank, ardent spirit, such as we may imagine marked the boyhood of such a man. When we recollect, too, the strong affection he always showed to this brother, we see plainly that the union of the two in one picture was rather the result of that known affection, than the act of the painter. This curious family and national picture bears about it every mark of its authenticity, and has never yet been engraved.

Amongst the remaining pictures, are—Philip, the fifth Earl of Leicester, by Kneller: Elizabeth, daughter of Col. Sidney, and wife of W. Perry, Esq., the same lady who figures in the large Perry family-piece just mentioned: Robert, Earl of Leicester, 1702, by Sir P. Lely: Elizabeth Egerton, Lady Leicester again, with a child, afterwards Lord Lisle, both by Lely: another Lady Leicester, a very fine, fair woman, with a profusion of brown hair: Christ at Emmaus, a large and good piece, by Jan Steen: Jane Wroth, Countess of Rochford, said to be by Netscher, *quere* by Lely? a fine woman, in Lely's style, with dark hair, hazel eyes, and large oval face, with an air of aristocratic dignity: Madonna and Child, by Leonardo da Vinci: portrait of a man, by Holbein, most capital and life-like: heads of Christ and Madonna, from the collection of Charles I., by Simon Mercati: rich man and Lazarus, by Bassan: several small family-pieces on copper, by Verelst: Flemish women, by Terburgh, excellent: Sir Thomas More, by Holbein: St. Lucia holding her eyes in a vase: the Flood, by Bassan: Holy Family, by Annibal Carracci: Barbara Gamage, first Countess of Leicester: Venus reclining, by Titian: head of a monk, by Perino del Vaga, with strong black hair, and features that would suit the Clerk of Copmanhurst: carving on wood, a saint at prayer, very excellent: Venus attired by the Graces, copied from Guido, by Lely: portrait of a lady, a lovely fair woman: martyrdom of St. Sebastian, a large piece, that wants cleaning: a small head of Martin Luther.

Such are the names of the greater number of the paintings at Penshurst. There are a good many, both family portraits and other paintings, by good masters, which are not, however, here mentioned; some few, too, were gone to be cleaned. I have desired to enumerate the majority, that persons of taste may be more aware, than has been the case, of the treasures of art hoarded in this venerable old house of the Sidneys : to attempt to discuss their respective merits is beyond the limits of this article; but it may be an additional inducement to those who would wish to visit Penshurst, from their reverence for those of its former inhabitants, who have done and suffered so much for the literature and the liberties of England, to know that they will not merely tread the same ground, and gaze on the same scenes as these patriots and heroes, but that these noble spirits have themselves collected for their recreation, works of art which would make the spot one of strong attraction, even if it were not hallowed by their memories, and embellished by all that remains of their presence— their pictured forms.

Few, I suspect, are aware how easy of access this interesting place is from the metropolis. In about three hours, and for a few shillings, a coach three times a week will set you down at an excellent inn on the very spot. From Tunbridge Wells, a few miles distant, this is now a favourite excursion, and the Dover Railway will, ere long, run through the vale of Tunbridge, so that we feel assured that Penshurst, standing as it does, in one of the most lovely districts of England, will be resorted to by a great multitude of our country-men.

At present, it is true, this interesting collection of paintings is in a state of much confusion. Both they and the building have evidently suffered seriously, not merely from time, but from neglect. In the great national changes, which since the days of the First Charles have passed over England, the great families and their houses have necessarily undergone ruinous changes too. Many such houses, at this moment, stand roofless and ivy-grown, never again to be restored. Others have only been recovered by the outlay of princely fortunes; and others still, though inhabited by the descendants of their ancient lords, bear about them, and will to the last, the marks of the scath and ravages which they have suffered. Penshurst is one of these; and no one who treads its silent park, and beholds its huge trees shattered by the tempests,—its grass-grown pleasaunce and its gray walls,—but will feel that it derives a stronger interest from these circumstances. It is not in a scene of entire modern gaiety and splendour that we would wish to come upon the domestic haunts of the Sidneys. Such a scene would violate all our ideas of the past, and disturb those feelings which drew us to the spot. We know that the

days of the Arcadia are gone by; we know that
Sir Philip Sidney died young on the field of
Zutphen, and Algernon's blood flowed on the
scaffold for the love of civil liberty; and a place
which bears on its face evidences of a kindred
fate, is just that which accords with our humour
at the moment, and deepens our impressions of the
past.   We do not expect to meet Ben Jonson
strolling through the park; or Waller and Saccharissa bandying compliments beneath the noble
beeches, now called Saccharissa's Walk; much
less do we expect to find Sir Philip pacing the
broad terrace of the garden, with his admired
sister Pembroke, and Edmund Spenser, deep in
dreams of chivalry and poetry, which no sound
of steam-engines, nor bruit of reform and regis-
trations, nor arrival of morning paper, in those
days disturbed.   All these things are of the past,
and of the fashion of the past which can never be
revived, and we love the spot which makes us
feel it.

Nothing, therefore, is more delightful than to see
the care which, in restoring this fine old fabric, has
been taken by its noble possessor, to preserve as
much of its antiquity as possible, and to build in the
spirit of it.   Lord de L'Isle is a worthy descendant
of the House of Sidney, and seems fully conscious

of the honour of such ancestry; it is therefore to be hoped, that in the course of improvement and restoration, a great deal will be done which yet needs it. I have already expressed the hope that the roof of the old banqueting hall will be repaired, and the hall thus be preserved to future generations, which, without speedy attention, will not outlast this.

It will be a worthy labour too, both as it regards the public and the works themselves, to have the paintings thoroughly cleaned, and disposed to best advantage. The family portraits should be arranged in chronological order; and when it is considered that the whole family is, with scarcely an exception, complete, it may be imagined how much the interest of the whole will be increased. When this is done, it will be difficult to call to mind a suite of ancient apartments, commencing with the old hall and terminating with the gallery, that will more completely transport the spectator into the stirring times of Elizabeth and the Commonwealth.

But there are other relics of the family at Penshurst. There are the MSS. In a cabinet, in one of the front rooms, is preserved a considerable collection of these. Some of their contents have been published, particularly those of a more political nature, in Collins's two volumes of the Sidney Papers. Mr. Blencowe has also published, in an-

other volume, under the same name, the Journal of
Robert, Earl of Leicester, father of Algernon, who
spent the troublous times of the civil wars and
commonwealth here, and regularly entered down
the passing events. We have also, in the same
volume, some letters of Algernon to his father and
others, all bearing the impress of the same high
and unbending spirit, perhaps the most perfect
image of Roman virtue that any modern state has
produced. Yet I have no doubt that a steady
inquest through those papers would discover much
matter that would interest the general reader. It
is not within the scope of such a work as this that
such materials could be comprehended. I can only
indicate their existence. It may, however, give
some idea of what might be found, to mention one
or two things that my eye casually fell upon. One
was a MS. with this title—

An. Dom. 1583.
Inventory of Household Furniture, etc. at Kenil-
worth Castle, belonging to Robert Dudley,
Earl of Leycester.
An. Dom. 1583.

What a volume this would have been for Sir Walter Scott when writing his romance of Kenil-worth! Here we have a thorough and particular account of the whole furnishing and household array of Kenilworth, at the very time at which Leicester gave his entertainment to the Queen. There is every article in the house from roof to cellar, and from the lady's bower to the stable. With this MS. before him, Sir Walter might have given us a portraiture of Kenilworth, not only as graphic as was his wont, but as true as if he had been at the entertainment himself. As it is, it is a most valuable exposition of the real state and fashion of a princely house in the reign of Elizabeth.

There are also two volumes of the Household Book of the Sidneys remaining. They are those of Algernon Sidney's father, and are thus entitled—

1624.

Household Expenses of the Right Honourable Lo. vicont Lisle, at London and Pencehurst,* from the xiii of Aprill unto xxi of March.

Expenses

In Kitchens, Larders, Buttrie, Sellers, Brewhouse,

* Still pronounced thus by the people thereabouts, evidently from the original name, Pencester.

Laundreys, Stables, fewell, and in other places,
As here-after may appeare.

In this book, as in the Household Book of the
Percys, which has been published, there is a most
exact and well-kept account of all expenses throughout the entire establishment. Of the methodical
and business habits of our great families in the
days of tilting and court revelry, nothing can give
more ample proof. Every thing is entered, and
every thing is valued. The accounts are not only
clear and minute, but they are set down in the
most leisurely and precise hand. Such accounts
were, no doubt, of the greatest value in their own
day, and to us they are not a whit the less so.
They are standing evidences, not only of what was
the consumption of a great house, and what were
the kind of articles used, but they give us the value
of every article of life at this period, and become data for any calculation of the change of
value in money and goods between that day and
this. We have meat, flour, eggs, fish, fowls, turkeys, pigs, wheat, oats, hay, brushes, mops, cloths,
etc. etc. all in their separate identity. There is no
lumping them in sundries. You see too what was

the peculiar style of serving the several tables kept in the house, for the old days of all dining in hall were over; there were, therefore, separate entries for every day and every room where a table was set. There was the lord's table; the table in the hall, probably for the steward, yeomen, and retainers; the kitchen for the kitchen servants; the nursery; and Algernon's room.

We find continual entries in 1625, "for Algernone," of puddings, birds, mutton, etc. If Algernon was born in 1622, as it has been asserted, he would now only be three years old, and would be in the nursery; but if in 1617, as is more probable, he would be eight, and thus at a more suitable age to be advanced to the dignity of a separate table. Whatever be the fact, these, however, and such, are the entries.

We find also that one day there is veal in the kitchen, mutton in the hall, and a capon in the nursery; the same general dishes seldom appearing at the different tables on the same day. Lord de L'Isle's eldest daughter, a fine lively girl of eleven, hearing us mention the nursery, was curious to know what the children of the family had two hundred years ago, and was amused to find that it was just what they themselves had had that day— a fowl.

In these books are duly entered the names of all the guests, so that by looking through them we can tell who were the visitants and associates of the family for thoŝe years. Many of these entries are very curious, as they regularly note how many attendants the guests brought, and how long they stayed. We may give a few samples, which are sufficiently indicative of the whole. Thus—

1624—Monday, 14th March.—At dinner, Lo. Percie and La. Percie; La. Carlisle; La. Maners; Sir Henry Lea; Mrs. Coulston.

At supper, Lord Percie, Ladie Delawar, and remaining a week.

Wednesday 16th, Lo. and La. went to Syon.

1625—12th of November.—Breakfast for La. Percie and La. Carlisle, and people going away.

Soon after occurs—Ladie Carlisle, with ten attendants, who staid fourteen days.

—Lord Wallingford; Lord Vauze; Sir Thos. Neville; Sir Antho. Forester; Lord Arundell; Sir Francis Smith; and their attendants after dinner.

—Thirty neighbours at dinner.

1625—30th December.—Sir Geo. and John Ryvers, and their La.; Mr. Geo. Ryvers; Justice

Dixon; Justice Selliard and his brethren; and Lord Cruckendon; Anthony Cambridge; and about thirty others at dinner. Prices of expenses for this weeke.—Kitchen, for flesh, fish, poultrie, butter, eggs, groceries, 29*l.* 17*s.* 10*d.*; Pantry and eller, in bread, beere, sack, claret, etc. 14*l.* 13*s.* 10*d.*; Brewhouse——Laundrie, soape and starge, 1*s.* 11*d.*; Stables, for hay and oats, 1*l.* 14*s.* 8*d.*; Fewell, in charcoal and billets, 3*l.* 9*s.*

This, it must be confessed, was jovial housekeeping, amounting to about 50*l.* for the week, or 2500*l.* the year, for mere eating and drinking, when a good pig was worth 1*s.* 8*d.*; and every thing in proportion.

These are striking testimonials to the truth of Ben Jonson's description in the poem already quoted, of the liberal and ungrudging hospitality of the Sidneys. Towards the alleviation of this cost we find continual entries of gifts from friends and tenants,—another fact also mentioned by Ben Jonson:

All come in, the farmer and the clowne,
And no one empty handed.

The singularity of the entry is, that even these gifts
have a value attached to them, as thus, in 1625:—
Gifts to the Lo. of Leycester: from the Earl of
Dorset, 1 stag, 2*l.*—from Goodman Edmunds, 1
pig, 1*s.* 8*d.*

There were also " Provision Rents," or rents
which probably small tenants paid in kind, which
came pouring in weekly, and must have proved
very comfortable apparitions to the cook, when
lords and ladies, with their troops of attendants,
rode clattering into court. These provision rents
are also regularly entered, and consisted of all
kinds of country produce,—bacon, fowls, turkeys,
geese, mutton, pigs—fat and sucking, fruits, corn,
cheese, butter, and such good things.

Besides these household books, and the volumes
of historical journals, political and literary, already
mentioned, there are some relating entirely to
family affairs, which must be very curious. I
observed a sort of summary of the historical reading of one of the earls, and a " Catalogue of the
Officers in the army of the Netherlands." This
was probably made by Robert Sidney, Sir Philip's
brother, who served in that army for some time.
I opened, too, " An account of the Ceremonials at
the Courts of Princes," evidently being a sort of
guide-book of one of the family while on foreign

embassage; probably that of the second earl, whose journal is published, and who was ambassador to France in the early part of Charles I.'s reign; with others which in the same manner indicate the countries and employments in which the writers or transcribers were engaged. There is one entitled, " The Meditations of the Countess of Bridgewater on eight chapters of Scripture." This was, no doubt, brought here by her daughter, Lady Elizabeth Egerton, the fourth Countess of Leicester.

These are all interesting peeps into the lives and characters of the various members of an ancient line, of some of whom no other memorial remains except the portrait on the wall. What can be more delightful than for the descendant of an old house to be able thus to unveil and make acquaintance with the thoughts and domestic feelings of his buried ancestors? We must not, however, leave this cabinet without noticing another article of its contents.

Of most of the distinguished personages of this family, a lock of hair has been carefully preserved, and they are here kept in little boxes. They have been severed from the head at various ages of the individual. Some have the infantine lightness of hue and silkiness of texture, and some are blanched with age. It was, however, a great pleasure to me

to see locks of the hair of Sir Philip and Algernon,
cut in the strength of their manhood, for they so
exactly agreed, both in character and colour with
that of their portraits in the house, as to give one
the most satisfactory idea of the scrupulous fidelity
of the painters.

We must here close our visit to Penshurst; only
adding, that in the church which stands near the
house, are to be found monuments of the Sidneys.
The remains of Sir Philip lie in St. Paul's Cathe-
dral. It may be interesting too, to lovers of our
history, to know that in the present parsonage, now
inhabited by the Rev. Philip Dodd and his daughter,
once dwelt Dr. Hammond, one of the chaplains
of Charles I., and author of various works of a
polemic or religious nature. In fact, the church,
the parsonage, the rustic churchyard—which is entered by an old-fashioned gateway through the
very middle of a house, and has some of its graves
planted with shrubs and flowers in the manner
which John Evelyn says was common in his time in
Surrey, the village, and the old mansion itself, are
all so pleasantly grouped on their gentle eminence,
and surrounded by so delightful a country, that
were there no other cause of attraction, it would
be difficult to point out a spot where the lovers of a
rural excursion, and a social party, could spend a

day more to their heart's desire. Who then would
not the more love to visit this spot for the recollections that cling to it?

> Are days of old familiar to thy mind,
> O reader? Hast thou let the midnight hour
> Pass unperceived, whilst thou in fancy lived
> With high-born beauties and enamoured chiefs,
> Sharing their hopes, and with a breathless joy
> Whose expectation touched the verge of pain,
> Following their dangerous fortunes? If such love
> Hath ever thrilled thy bosom, thou wilt tread,
> As with a pilgrim's reverential thoughts,
> The groves of Penshurst. Sidney here was born.
>   SOUTHEY.

Yes, in these scenes you seem to make human acquaintance, even though ages and death and decay
are between you, with spirits that were before unto
you merely after the fashion of Ariel,—coming, indeed, at your call, from the fairy-land of books,
and singing to you unearthly melodies, but having
no local habitation. Here you have before you the
traces and evidences of their humanity. Here you
see Sir Philip Sidney, as the boy and the man;
you walk under his oak; you tread with Ben Jonson beneath the mighty chestnuts still crowning the
hills of the park; you pace under the stupendous

beeches of Saccharissa's Walk, now battered with
time and tempests; you see Algernon Sidney, not
merely as the stern patriot, planning the overthrow
of monarchy, but as the delicate child of a stately
line daintily fed in his separate chamber; you recognize the Fair Pembroke as a daughter of this
house; and everywhere tokens of the visits and
favour of Edward VI., of Elizabeth, and James,
bring us back in spirit to those remarkable reigns.
Numbers of portraits of those who figured most
eminently on the political stage then, complete the
impression; and we cannot bid adieu to the venerable pile of Penshurst without feeling that it has
not merely afforded us a deep satisfaction, but has
stimulated us to a closer acquaintance with some
of the proudest characters and most eventful times
of English history.

VISIT TO THE FIELD OF CULLODEN.

THERE are few things more interesting than a visit to an old battle-field. The very circumstance impresses indelibly on your mind the history connected with it. It awakes a more lively interest about the deeds done there, than the mere meeting with them in a book can. It kindles a curiosity about all the persons and the events that once passed over it; and when you have inquired, the living knowledge which you have gained of the place and its localities, fixes the facts for ever in your memories.

Besides that, old traditions linger about the field and its vicinity, which in the excitement of the main transaction never found their way into the record. There are passages, and glimpses of personages, that the historian did not learn, or did not deign to place on his page, which have nevertheless a vivid effect on the heart and the imagination of him who wanders and muses there in after time. You see, even long ages afterwards, evidences of the wrath and ravages of the moment of contention,

and touching traces of those human sufferings,
which, though they make the mass of instant
misery and the most fruitful subject of subsequent
reflection, are lost in the glare of worldly glory,
and the din of drums and trumpets. You see where
the fierce agency of fire and artillery have left
marks of their rage—where they have shivered
rocks and shattered towers, laid waste dwellings
and blown up the massy fortresses of the feudal
ages. Nature, with all her healing and restoring
care, does not totally erase or conceal these.
There are gray crumbling walls, weed-grown
heaps, grassy mounds shrouding vast ruins; and
even at times, of the slaughtered hosts, still

> The graves are green ; they may be seen.

Of the battle-fields in this country, I know none
which have more interested my imagination than
those of Flodden and Culloden. Both were pecu-
liarly disastrous to Scotland : in one the king was
slain with nearly all his nobility, in the other the
regal hopes of his unfortunate descendants were
extinguished for ever. These circumstances have
made them both themes of poetry and romance of
the highest quality which Scotland has ever produced. No one can read the pathetic ballad—

> The flowers of the forest are all wede away,

without feeling a strong interest in Flodden; and the vast influence which the battle of Culloden has had on the fortunes of this country, render the spot on which it was fought one of peculiar note to. Englishmen. It was there that the fate of the Stuart dynasty was sealed. It was there that it was demonstrated beyond dispute, that any chance of that family—so unfortunately attached to principles of government and religion which the bulk of the empire rejected and abjured,—to regain the throne of these kingdoms, was gone for ever. It was there that popery and regal despotism, as regnant powers in Great Britian, were destroyed. It was there that not only was Protestantism made triumphant, but that the empire was consolidated far more than by the formal Act of Union itself. While the Highlands continued the stronghold of Jacobitism, there was a weak place in the kingdom which France and Spain were only too well acquainted with; and on any recurrence of hostility with them, we were threatened with invasion and insurrection at once. The course of the rebellion of 1745, which was terminated at Culloden, by showing the hopelessness of such attempts, put an end to them. It was found that the Highlanders alone, out of the immense population of the realm, could be roused to assert the claims of the old dynasty, and the battle of Culloden laid the Highlands at the feet of the conquerors, and they were crushed into passive obedience.   Henceforward all parties, English and Scotch, highlanders and lowlanders, have felt so vitally the advantages of union; of one common empire, and one common interest; and such has been the manifest progress in wealth, and power, and knowledge, of Britian—sound, and whole, and healthy in all its members, and with the same political and commercial advantages accessible to all its children, that every one must rejoice in the course which events have taken.   Instead of internal divisions and squabbles about the crown, laying her open to attacks from without, Britian by her union has advanced to an eminence amongst the nations, most glorious in itself, and to a prospect of political dominion and moral influence that have no parallel, and that are too vast even for the strongest imagination to embrace.

On the other hand, putting out of view these considerations and consequences, history has few things so striking as the transactions that terminated at Culloden.   We see an ancient dynasty driven from the throne of a splendid empire, striving to regain it, and that particular race from which it sprang, adhering with inviolable devotion to its fortunes; and ready, in the face of millions, and the vast resources of England, to stand to the death for its claims. Nothing can be more picturesque and heroic than the Highlanders, as seen in this history. Their magnificent mountain-land, their peculiar costume, their clanship, their whole life and character, so different to those of the rest of the empire, all add their effect to that romantic valour which, on the appearance of Prince Charles, burst forth over the vales of England, struck terror into the heart of the metropolis, and then, as suddenly retreating, expired in one melancholy blaze on the Field of Culloden.

It is no wonder that the struggles of the exiled Stuarts, and the exploits of the Highlanders, have produced such a multitude of Jacobite songs, and such romances as those of Scott; and, as thousands of our countrymen and countrywomen now traverse every summer the very scenes inhabited by these heroic clans, and where the principal events of the last rebellion took place, it may be as well, before describing the visit to Culloden, to take a hasty glance at the events that so fatally terminated there.

The moment that our summer tourists enter the

great Caledonian Canal, one of the most magnificent, and now one of the most accessible routes
which they can take, they are in the very cradle
of the Rebellion of *forty-five*. Right and left of
those beautiful lochs over which they sail, in the
glens and recesses of the wild hills around them,
dwell the clans that carried such alarm into England. The fastnesses of Lochabar, Moidart, and
Badenoch, sent forth their mountaineers at the first
summons of their Prince. Not a splintered mountain towers in view, nor a glen pours its waters
into the Glen More nan Albin, or Great Glen of
Scotland, but bears on it some trace or tradition
of those times. Fort William, Fort Augustus, the ·
shattered holds of Inverlochy, Invergary, Glen
Moriston, all call them to your remembrances. It
was here that Lochiel called them around the
standard of Charles; it was here they gathered in
their strength, and drove out every Saxon, except
the garrison of Fort William ; and it was here that
the troops of the bloody Duke of Cumberland came
at his command, and blasted the whole region with
fire and sword. It is wonderful how nature, in
ninety years, can so completely have reclothed the
valleys with wood, and turned once more that
black region of the shadow of death into so smiling
a paradise. When you ascend to the justly cele-

brated Fall of Foyers, you are again reminded of forty-five, by passing the house of Frazer of Foyers; and as you approach Inverness, you only get nearer to the startling catastrophe of the drama. Your whole course has been through the haunts of the Camerons, the Macdonalds, the Grants, the Macphersons, and Frazers, the rebel clans of forty-five, —and it leads you, as it did them, to the Muir of Culloden.

From the first commencement of the troubles of the house of Stuart to the last effort in their behalf, the Highlanders were their firm, and it may be said almost their only friends. The lowland Scots, incensed at the attempt of Charles I. to impose the English liturgy upon them, were amongst the earliest to proclaim the solemn league and covenant, and to join the English Parliament against him; but the Highlanders, under Montrose, rose in his cause, and created a powerful diversion in his favour. Again, when Charles the II. attempted a similar measure and aroused a similar spirit in the lowlands, the Highlanders, under the celebrated Claverhouse, maintained the royal ordinance; and again, under the same commander, fought for James II. against his successful rival William III. In George II.'s reign, in 1715, they once more, under the Earl of Mar, set up the standard of the

Pretender, part of them marching as far as Preston in Lancashire, where they were compelled to lay down their arms, while the remainder were defeated by the Duke of Argyle. Finally, they made their most brilliant, but ultimately fatal attempt, in 1745, under Prince Charles Edward. Thus, for upwards of a hundred years they maintained their attachment, and were ready to shed their blood, for the fallen race of their ancient kings. So desperate, as it regarded all other aid, was become the Stuart cause, that Charles, when he landed on the west coast of Scotland in 1745, was attended only by seven men. If the hand of Providence was ever revealed against the success of any cause, through the agency of the elements, it was most signally against that of the Stuarts. Great was the admiration at the destruction of the Spanish armada in the reign of Elizabeth, chiefly by a tempest; but scarcely, for more than a century, did a ship or a fleet issue from the ports of Spain or France, to further the designs of the Stuarts on England, but it was struck upon the rocks, or blown adrift and scattered by a storm, or instantly encountered by a hostile force. In 1715, a vessel, with arms and money, sent by the French king to the aid of the Highlanders under Mar, was wrecked and totally lost on the coast of Scotland. In 1719, a fleet of ten ships of the line, with several frigates, having on board 6000 troops, and 12,000 stand of arms, was sent out from Cadiz by the court of Spain, to assert the claim of the Pretender in England—it was completely dispersed by a violent storm off Cape Finisterre! In the beginning of the year 1744, Charles was summoned from Rome to accompany Marshal Saxe, with a French army of 13,000 men, to England. The court and people of England were greatly alarmed,* and not without cause, for most of the British troops were in Flanders; the grand fleet of England was in the Mediterranean; and there were only six ships of the line ready for sea, lying at Spithead. But the elements once more rose against the Stuarts. As Marshal Saxe and the young Pretender were busy embarking their troops, the wind changed to the east, and blew a storm: several transports were wrecked; a good many troops and seamen perished; a great quantity of warlike stores were lost; an English fleet was mustered from the different ports of the Channel, and the enterprise was abandoned.

Spite of this warring of the elements against his family, in the following spring he embarked in a

* Home's History of the Rebellion, vol. i. p. 32.

7*

frigate of sixteen guns, called the Doutelle, accompanied by an old man-of-war, the Elizabeth, of
sixty guns. They had not sailed far when they
met an English man-of-war, the Lyon, which engaged the Elizabeth, and so disabled her as to
compel her to put back to port, and Charles proceeded in his little frigate, with seven adventurers
and a sum of money somewhat less than 4000*l.*
He reached the Western Isles, but was refused aid
by the chiefs. He landed at Moidart; erected his
standard in Glen-Finnan; the Highlanders rose
around him, and soon set forward with him on the
most daring and adventurous enterprise that ever
was undertaken,—no other than to hurl his Hanoverian rival from the British throne, and set his
own father upon it. Their success speedily asto-
nished all Europe. They marched to Edinburgh,
and took possession of it. The Prince took up his
quarters in Holyrood, the ancient palace of his
ancestors, and proclaimed his father king. He
marched out, and defeated the English forces
at Preston-Pans, with a facility and a total rout
that appeared miraculous. His victorious army,
amounting to less than 6000 men, marched forward to invade England. The people of London
soon heard with consternation and amazement
that they had taken Carlisle, occupied Penrith,

Kendal, Lancaster, Manchester; and finally, in only thirteen days from their leaving Edinburgh, were quartered in Derby.   Nothing could exceed the terror of the metropolis.   The moneyed men were struck with a deadly panic; numbers got together what property they could and fled into the country; several vessels lay at the Tower quay, ready to convey the king and his treasures to Hanover; the Duke of Newcastle, the prime minister, shut himself up alone for two days, deliberating whether he should avow himself for the Stuart line, or not.   It is true that an army of 30,000 men, chiefly of militia, lay at Finchley, and the Duke of Cumberland, with another army, was hovering near the Highlanders on the edge of Staffordshire; but such was the opinion of the desperate valour of the Scots, and such were the spirits of the Scots themselves, that the Chevalier Johnstone, who was in the Prince's army, and commonly blames him for rashness, expresses his persuasion that had he then pushed on to London, the Finchley army would have melted away, and the crown might now have been on a Stuart's head.

But such was not the fortune of that line.   The chiefs, struck with a sense of their own temerity, and with the fact that none of the English joined them, resolved to retreat northward, to the cruel

chagrin of both Prince and soldiers. They made
a retreat as extraordinary as their march had been.
With the Duke of Cumberland now hotly pursuing,
they yet pushed on without loss or molestation, except at Clifton in Cumberland, where they speedily
repulsed the Duke's troops. They reached Falkirk,
and there mustering 8000 men, they attacked and
completely routed the English army under General
Hawley, 13,000 in number. The chiefs, still deem-
ing it prudent to retreat, contrary to the Prince's
judgment, they now reached Inverness, doomed to
be the scene of the termination of this most extraordinary and meteorlike adventure. Prince
Charles has been charged both by friends and foes
with rashness and cowardice. The history of
Home, who served in the army opposed to him,
certainly does not warrant any charge of cowardice ; and if that of rashness be better founded, it
should be recollected that Charles Edward had
been for years amused with promises of assistance
from France to regain the crown—promises that
ended in nothing ; that the prize aimed at was a
noble one ; that he had seen nothing but victory
attend him, and the throne at one moment apparently all but achieved. That he had been irritated—being forced on retreat after retreat by his
own officers, over four successive fields of victory

—and that now they proposed a further retreat
into the mountains. These must be taken as pallia-
tives; yet his conduct now was rash to madness,
and cost him the destruction of his cause. The
troops were worn out with their long and wonderful march. They were famished for want of
provisions. They had had no pay for six weeks;
and the bulk of them were dispersed, seeking rest
and refreshment amongst their friends and families.
These circumstances all pointed to the course
which his chiefs counselled, to avoid a general engagement, and assume a strong position in the
mountains. The evil angel of the Stuart race prevailed. Charles harassed his men by a miserable
night march in a vain attempt to surprise Cumberland's camp; and when the worn-out and starving
soldiers had just thrown themselves down in the
neighbouring woods, and under the walls on Culloden Moor to sleep, the Duke was upon them. It is
melancholy to imagine those brave men, who had
shown such unparalleled devotion, and had performed such wonders, thus forced to go into battle,
faint with want of food, of rest, and sleep, with
scarcely half of their numbers assembled.* The

* The number of Highlanders in the battle of Culloden was
about 5000; of the king's troops nearly double that amount.

English artillery swept them down by whole ranks, and they were speedily seen flying in all directions. The fate of the Stuart dynasty was sealed for ever, and the bloody butcheries of the monster Cumberland were then to begin.

Thinking and talking over " this strange eventful history," we set out from the interesting town of Inverness,* to walk to Culloden Moor, on Thursday the 11th of August, 1836—just ninety years and about three months after the occurrence of that memorable battle, it being fought on the 16th of April, 1746.

We found it a pleasant ramble of about four miles; partly amid pleasant cultivated fields, with their corn ripe for the harvest; partly along the

* Inverness is one of the most delightful and interesting places in the kingdom. Delightful from its fine situation, on the margin of the Murray Frith, and surrounded by mountain regions of the greatest beauty. It is interesting by its numerous poetical and historical associations. Being the capital of the Highlands, it is full of clan history. Almost every object on which your eye falls has its peculiar recommendation—such as the old castle of Macbeth, where he murdered the king; Craig Phadric, a wild hill crowned with one of those vitrified forts that have so much puzzled the antiquaries; Tomnaheurich, or the Hill of the Fairies, a very singular hill, said to be the burial-place of Thomas the Rhymer, etc. etc.

shore of the Murray Frith; and partly through woods of Scotch fir.   As we approached Culloden, we asked many of the peasantry living near the wood whether we were in the right direction, but not one could speak English.   The ground gradually ascended as we advanced, and when we came in sight of the Moor, we found a sort of observatory tower built by the gentleman who now lives in Culloden House, and a number of old cannons lying about, evidently intended to give the place a fortified air; one of those whims which so frequently seize people in picturesque situations, but of which the interest dies before the object is finished.   We were now speedily on the Moor, and were at a loss whether to admire more the black and blasted aspect of this fatal spot, or the magnificent scenery of which it is the melancholy centre.   To the south, beyond the river Nairn, rose wild ranges of hills which run into the mountains of Badenoch; to the north lay at our feet the Murray Frith, to the right showing Fort George, built on a narrow promontory pushing into it from the southern shore, and on the opposite shore Fort Rose; to our left lay the dark woods and green hills between us and Inverness, and all before us one wide and splendid prospect,—the mountain re-

gions of Rosshire, with Ben Wyvers lifting his
cloudy bulk far above the rest.

Between us and the Murray Frith ran a narrow
strip of cultivated country, and just below us appeared, shrouded in its solemn woods, Culloden
House, at the time of the Rebellion the residence
of the celebrated Lord Forbes of Culloden, President of the Court of Session; a man whose advice,
had it been taken, would, in all probability, have
prevented the Rebellion, and whose exertions actually broke it of so much of its force that its
defeat may be attributed to him more than to any
other cause.*   The Moor itself, on which we stood,

* The heavy Dutch and Hanoverian kings whom it was
the fortune of this kingdom to have subsequently to the
expulsion of the Stuarts, never seemed to have the slightest
conception that their rule might be made popular by concilia-
tion and kindness.   The Highlanders, who were the most to
be feared in case of any attempt of the Stuarts to regain the
crown, were treated uniformly with contempt or asperity.
In 1738, Lord Forbes, when a war with Spain was expected,
represented to Sir Robert Walpole, through Lord Milton and
the Earl of Ilay, that the first thing which Spain would do
would be to excite the Highlanders; but that all that danger
might be most easily prevented by raising four or five Highland regiments, and giving commissions in them to their
chiefs.   Sir Robert expressed his admiration of the plan,

we found as Robert Chambers in his Picture of Scotland has correctly stated, " a vast table-land covered with heath, over which are scattered a few wretched cottages." These cottages, however, are chiefly sprinkled over that side of the Moor nearest to Inverness, with their little patches of corn and potatoes, and give some aspect of life and cultivation to the scene; but the site of the battle itself, and the heath far beyond, are as free from the marks of culture as they could be in the days of Adam. In the words of the same worthy and indefatigable authority, " the whole plain is as desolate and blasted in appearance as if it suffered under a curse, or were conscious of the blood which it had drank." It is, in fact, in strict poetical keeping with our feelings on visiting such a place. Culloden Moor ought to be Culloden Moor; not a mere common-place tract of pasturage or corn-field. Old battle fields are the property of the nation; they are spots bearing evidence to the changes of our dynasties, and the conflicts, good or evil, through which England has passed to what she now is. However, therefore,

wondered that it had never before occurred to any one, and warmly recommended it in council. The scheme was rejected, and in seven years after came the Rebellion.

farmers and country squires, and political economists may rave at our folly, we cannot help being
jealous of the rooting out with the plough and the
spade, the identifying marks of our national battle-
fields. The greater part of the scenes of these
great conflicts, of which we read in English history, we find, on visiting, so exactly like the other
fields of hay and corn around them, that we have
a difficulty in realizing to ourselves that these are
actually the sites of those great actions that stand
so prominently in our annals. Even Flodden is a
corn-field; and the hill on which James V. posted
himself, is at present fast disappearing to mend the
roads. But Culloden is every thing that the poet
or the antiquary would wish it to be. It is solemn
and melancholy as the imagination of the most
sympathetic visiter can desire: and who does not
sympathize with the fate of so many brave men,
who had burst forth in so romantic an enterprise
for the restoration of their fallen kings, and had
done such extraordinary deeds in it? Who can
avoid sympathizing in the last vain efforts of a
high-spirited people to mantain their independence
against a nation of such overwhelming power as
England, notwithstanding the misgovernment of
the Stuarts, and the clear demonstration, from that
day to this, that their removal from the throne was

one of the most auspicious events that ever happened to this kingdom ?

Though ninety years have passed since the battle of Culloden, the field is covered with the marks
of that day.   The moment you set foot on the
scene of action, you recognize every position of
the contending armies, and the objects which surrounded them.   The night before the battle, Prince
Charles and his officers lodged in Culloden House.
There stands Culloden, restored and beautified
since then, but occupying the same site and surrounded by the same wood.   The battle took place
between this house and an extensive inclosure on
the Moor, the north wall of which screened the
right flank of the Highland army.   This wall the
English troops partly pulled down, and raked the
flank of the rebels with such a murderous fire of
artillery as cut down almost every man, and
caused the almost instantaneous rout of the right
wing.   The mouldering remains of that old and
shattered wall still stretch across the Moor in the
very course laid down in the original plans of the
battle.   In the centre of the place of action the .
ground was hollow and boggy.   The ground is
now sound, but you see plainly the hollow extent
of the morass.

To the south-west stood, at that day, a large

farm-house, called Balvraid; to this house the right
wing of the rebels retreated; here great numbers
of their comrades gathered to them, and in a body
made good, and indeed without pursuit, their way
into Badenoch. The house stands there yet. On
the northern edge of the battle field, near the extremity of the left wing, is marked the site of a
hut: this was unquestionably the hut of a blacksmith, the only house then standing precisely on the
battle field. This smith, so says the current tradition of the place, was a stalwart fellow, but not at
all desirous to take part in the fray, but the Highlanders compelled every man that they found in
the vicinity to come forth to their help. Their
numbers were diminished by absence, and their
strength by starvation and excessive fatigue; they
needed all aid that they could command, and they
insisted on the jolly smith taking arms. The smith
was very loath and very dogged, but, snatching up
the shaft of a cart that was reared against the
wall of his smithy, he took his post beside them.
When, however, he saw the havoc made by the
English cavalry amongst his countrymen, his blood
was up, and rushing into the thickest of the fray,
he laid about him with his tremendous weapon,
knocking down the troopers from their horses, and
levelling all that he came near. The exploits of

this son of Vulcan turning the attention of the cavalry on him, he was beset by overwhelming numbers, and after performing prodigies of valour, and laying low many with his cart shaft, he was at length compelled to fly. He took the road towards Inverness, the direction which the greater number of the fugitives were taking, and after turning repeatedly on his pursuers, and bringing down several of them, he was at length killed, not far from the mill, about a mile from Inverness, where the last bodies were found. The country people yet tell the spot where the sturdy blacksmith dropped. His smithy stood from year to year on the fatal field, deserted and gradually falling to decay. It remained a heap of smouldering ruin till within these few years, when several fresh huts springing up on the Moor not far off, the people gradually conveyed away the stones of the walls to construct their own habitations. It is said that the forge, the tools, and heaps of rusty iron, were found beneath the ruins of the roof which had fallen in. Such had been the horror connected with that fatal field, that none had cared to carry them away. When we saw the place every stone was grubbed up to the bottom of the foundation, and a pool of water nearly filled the hollow; but you had only to turn up any part of the floor

8*

which was bare, and you found it to consist of the cinders and smithy-slack of the brave old blacksmith's forge.

A road has been cut across the Moor since the battle, which passes right through the centre of the scene of action, and runs close past the site of the smith's forge; and it passes, too, amid what are the most striking and conspicuous objects on the field —the graves of the slaughtered soldiers. Nothing can be more impressive than these graves. The whole Moor besides is one black waste of heath; but these graves are grassy mounds of clear green, the only green spot within the whole compass of the melancholy Moor. They lie right and left of the road, but principally on the south side. The road, as we observed, having been cut across the heath since the battle, and passing directly across the place of graves, has no doubt covered some of them for ever from our view, but has brought the remainder under the very eye of all that travel through Culloden. Burns once looked on these green hillocks in his northern ramble, and described his own and the popular feeling in

THE LOVELY LASS OF INVERNESS.

The lovely lass o' Inverness,
Na joy nor pleasure can she see;

For e'en and morn she cries alas!
And ay the saut tear blins her e'e :—

" Drumossie Moor,* Drumossie day,
 A waefu' day it was to me !
 For there I lost my father dear,
 My father dear and brethren three.

" Their winding-sheet the bloody clay,
 Their graves are growing green to see ;
 And by them lies the dearest lad
 That ever blest a woman's e'e !

" Now wae to thee, thou cruel lord,
 A bloody man I trow thou be ;
 For many a heart thou hast made sair,
 That ne'er did wrang to thine or thee."

That we might not miss any information connected with the spot, we entered a hut not very far
from the old smith's forge, and to our great satisfaction found a family that could speak English.
They were, a widow of the name of Mackenzie,
and her son and daughter, both grown up. They
appeared very intelligent, and took a warm interest in every thing relating to the field of battle.
They told us that some of their family had lived on

* Drumossie was the old name of Culloden.

this spot from the day of the contest. That, besides
the smith's hut, this was the only one in the immediate vicinity of the field. That it had been called
Stable Hollow ever since, from a number of the
English troopers after the fight putting up their
horses in the shed belonging to it, while they went
to strip the slain. That their ancestors, the occupiers of the cottage, all made their escape, with the
exception of one young man who was compelled by
the Highlanders to go into the battle. That such
was his horror and frenzy, when he saw the flight
and bloody havoc that took place, that he flew
across the field without knowing whither he was
going, and was not heard of for more than two
months, when he most unexpectedly again made
his appearance, wasted almost to a skeleton. They
had supposed him killed in the battle. They afterwards learned that he had been roving amongst
the hills of Badenoch, in a state of apparent idiocy;
and only saved from starvation by the pity of the
inhabitants. Of this, however, he himself could
give no account, nor did he ever afterwards regain
his former tone of mind.

William, or as they called him, Wully Mackenzie,
the widow's son, was a short strong-built youth of
about twenty years of age; he was a gardener by
trade, and as well informed as Scotch gardeners

generally are. We were particularly pleased with the openness and intelligence of his countenance, and on his part he offered with great evidence of pleasure to conduct us over the field. He pointed out to us a large stone, not far from their cottage; *i. e.* on the north side of the scene of action, and on the left wing of the Highland army, where tradition said that a French engineer had posted his artillery, and committed considerable havoc on the English line. When we reached the graves, he directed our attention to a little stream that wandered through the heath near them, and a spring which was before the battle particularly admired for its delicious water. During the contest a number of the wounded crawled to it to assuage their thirst; and amongst them an officer who, as he was just raising his head, again was struck with a ball, and fell with his head into the spring. There, after the battle, he was found; the fountain itself perfectly choked up with the stiffened corses of himself and the heaps of combatants that had fallen there. From that day to the present, he said, nobody would ever drink from that spring; and in truth it was nearly overgrown with long grass and weeds, that testified to its not being disturbed by visitants.

As we sate on the greensward of one of these

battle-graves, we observed that in many places the
turf had been broken up by digging; and our
young guide told us that scarcely a party came
there but was desirous to carry away the fragment
of a bone as a relic. " What," said we, " are the
bones soon come at?" " Yes," he replied, " in
some places they lie within a foot of the surface."
These graves have been dug into in hundreds of
places, yet you can scarcely turn a turf but you
come upon them.   He dug out a sod with his
knife, and throwing out a little earth, presently
came to fragments of the crumbling bones of the
skeletons of 1746.   He told us that in one instance,
a quantity of bones which had been carried off by
a traveller, had been sent back at a great expense,
and buried again; the person who conveyed them
away being continually tormented by his con-
science and his dreams, till this was done; " and
the next visiter," added Wully Mackenzie, " would
most probably carry them off once more."   Balls
and portions of military accoutrements are still not
unfrequently found about the heath.   We picked
up as we walked across it, a leaden bullet, flattened
by having struck against some hard body and rendered quite white with age.

" Many a clever fellow lies here!" said young
Mackenzie, as he was busy turning up the sod in

quest of some appearance of bones; and indeed
what a contrast was that quiet scene, with the sun
and breeze of August playing over it, to what it
was ninety years before, when these dry bones
lived! In such situations we often, and very
naturally, wish that we could call up some of the
dead to tell us what were their thoughts and feelings in that moment of wrath and confusion; but
we had no need of that here. All those who were
now reduced beneath our feet to dust and mouldering bones, had left their representatives behind
them, to tell us not only what they had suffered,
but what the surviving Highlanders suffered.
Many who fought in that battle, have left more or
less some written account of it; but remarkably
enough, an officer of each contending army has
been the historian of the whole war. Home in the
king's army, and the Chevalier Johnstone in that
of the prince, have left us vivid records of the field
of Culloden, and all that led to it, and all that followed it. The escape, and wanderings of Prince
Charles for more than five months through the
Highlands, with the king's soldiers after him, with
the price of 30,000*l.* set upon his head, and the
peremptory orders of the Duke of Cumberland to
put him to death the instant he was found—his
living in the cave in the wild mountain Coramhian,

with the seven Macdonalds—his escape by Captain
Mackenzie personating him, and sacrificing his life
for him; the adventure of Flora Macdonald, the
prototype of Scott's Flora Mac Ivor, who rescued
him from his pursuers in one of the Western Isles,
by conveying him away disguised as her Irish
maid Betty Burke,—all these things, from their
own romantic nature, and the rank of the person
concerned, have been made familiar to all readers.
The narrative of the escape of the Chevalier Johnstone, however, as written by himself, is to the full,
in my opinion, as interesting, because it may be
considered as the recital of one out of the multitude
of those who fled from Culloden for their lives—
some to escape by a hair's-breadth, but many more
to perish by the sword of the pursuer, or the scaffold, as Kilmarnock, Balmerino, old Lovat, and
their fellows, whose heads so long dried in the
winds on Temple Bar and London Bridge.*

* The Chevalier Johnstone's history is a romance of real
life, to the full as interesting, and abounding with hair-
breadth escapes, as the tales of the author of Waverley; and,
indeed, frequently reminds you of his characters and incidents. The chevalier was the only son of James Johnstone,
merchant in Edinburgh. His family, by descent and alliance,
was connected with some of the first houses in Scotland.
His sister Cecilia was married to a son of Lord Rollo, who

One cannot even now, nearly a century after its enactment, traverse this last field of the Jacobite wars, without a strong feeling for all the human suffering in which this bloody drama closed; but

succeeded to the title and estate in 1765. The chevalier moved in the best society of the Scottish capital, and was treated by the then celebrated Lady Jane Douglas with the tenderness of a parent. Educated in Episcopalian and Jacobite principles, on the first intelligence of the landing of Prince Charles Edward, he made his escape from Edinburgh to the seat of Lord Rollo, near Perth, where he waited the arrival of the Prince, and was one of the first low-country gentlemen that joined his standard. He acted as aid-de-camp to Lord George Murray, and also to the Prince; and after the battle of Preston-Pans, he received a captain's commission, and bore a part in all the movements of the rebel army till the defeat at Culloden. From Culloden he escaped with the utmost peril to Killihuntly, where Mrs. Gordon, the lady of the house, offered to build him a hut in the mountains, and give him a few sheep to look after, so that he might pass for a shepherd; but the uneasiness of his mind would not allow him to adopt such a life. He fled to Rothiemurchus, where the young laird advised him to surrender himself to the government, as he had advised others, particularly Lord Balmerino; advice which, had he adopted it, would have caused his destruction, as it did theirs. From house to house, and place to place, he escaped by the most wonderful chances and under all sorts of disguises. He passed continually amongst the English soldiers busy at their work of devastation, his blood boiling with fury at the sight, but instant death his fate if he gave still stronger is that of indignant contempt for that monster Cumberland. It was impossible not to reflect what was the shocking barbarity with which he treated many of those whose bones now moul-

one sign of his feelings. Seventeen days he remained in the house of a very poor peasant, called Samuel, in Glen-Prossen; Samuel's daughter watching at the entrance of the glen. He was determined to reach Edinburgh if possible, and thence escape to England, and so to the Continent; but chances were a hundred to one against him. Every part of the country was overrun with soldiers, every outlet was watched, and heavy penalties denounced on any boatman who conveyed a rebel across the Tay and Forth. He prevailed, however, with two young ladies to ferry him over the Tay; but after a dreadful journey on foot into Fifeshire, he found the utmost difficulty in getting across the Forth to Edinburgh. The account of his negotiations and disappointments at Dubbie-sides, where no fisherman would carry him over; but where he did at length get carried over by a young gentleman and a drunken fisher, is very much in the Waverley manner. After being concealed with an old nurse at Leith, and partly with Lady Jane Douglas at Drumshcagh—he set out for England as a Scotch pedlar, on a pony. On his way he encountered a Dick Turpin sort of gentleman, and again a mysterious personage, who entered the inn where he was near Stamford, seated himself at table with him, and after playing away heartily at a piece of cold veal, began to interrogate him about the rebels in Scotland. Escaping from this fellow by the sacrifice of some India handkerchiefs, he got to London, where he lay concealed for a long time amongst his friends—fell dered beneath our feet. " The Duke of Cumberland," says the Chevalier Johnstone, " had the cruelty to allow our wounded to remain amongst the dead on the field of battle, stript of their clothes, from Wednesday, the day of our unfortunate engagement, till three o'clock on Friday; when he sent detachments to kill all those who were still in life; and a great many, who had resisted the effects of the continual rains which fell all that time, were then dispatched. He ordered a barn, which contained many of the wounded Highlanders, to be set on fire; and having stationed soldiers round it, they with fixed bayonets drove back the unfortunate men who attempted to save themselves, into the flames; burning them alive in this horrid manner, as if they had not been fellow-

into a very interesting love adventure—and saw many of his comrades pass his window on their way to execution. On one occasion he was invited by his landlord as a relaxation, to go and see two rebels executed on Tower Hill, Lords Kilmarnock and Balmerino! He finally escaped to Holland, in the train of his friend Lady Jane Douglas; entered into the service of France, went to Louisbourg in America, and returned to France to poverty and old age! Such is one recorded life of a Jacobite of the expedition of forty-five,— how many such, and even more wretched, passed unrecorded!

creatures."* This was a fitting commencement of those dreadful atrocities which he perpetrated in the country of the rebellious clans. The burnings, massacres, violations, and other demoniacal outrages with which he laid waste some of the most beautiful regions on the globe; deeds which will make his name infamous while there is a human feeling, or the power to record it in the world.

As we left the field, we gave, with our thanks, a small gratuity to our intelligent young guide, Wully Mackenzie, which seemed to him so much beyond his services, that, in the height of his gratitude, he was quite uneasy that he could not show us some further good office. " Was there nothing more that he could do? Would we go in and sit down to rest us awhile? Would we like a tune on the bagpipes?" As it is always a pleasure to gratify a generous feeling, in we went, and took our seats in their little hut, a regular Highland habitation, with smoky rafters, while Wully produced his pipes, and began to put them in order. There is something very delightful to sit in the simple cabin of these mountaineers, and see them converse with an easy and unembarrassed air, and with a mixture of intelligence and local superstition nowhere else to be

* Memoirs of the Rebellion, p. 146.

found. We observed that the beds, and various parts of the roof, were canopied with birch boughs, which had dried with all their leaves on. These, they assured us, were a certain protection from the plague of flies, for not a fly would go near the birch. This, we suppose, is a fact which experience has taught them, and if so, is a valuable one. We had a long talk with these good people, about the battle-field and its traditions. They told us that the name of Drumossie was not now used for that Moor—Culloden had superseded it; but was retained on a wild track at its extremity in the direction of Badenoch. They assured us, with the utmost gravity, that a battle would some day be fought *there*. We inquired how they knew that. They replied, that it had been repeatedly seen. On a summer's evening, people going across that moor had suddenly on various occasions found themselves in the very midst of the smoke and noise of a battle. They could see the various clans engaged, and clearly recognize them by their proper tartans; and on all these occasions the Laird of Culdethel, a neighbouring gentleman, was conspicuous on his white horse. One woman was so frightened and bewildered by this strange spectacle that she fainted away, and on coming to herself, found all traces of the battle gone, and made the best of her way home again without proceeding on her original object. We told them that these must be strong impressions left on the imaginations of the people by the memory of the old battle, but they only skook their heads. They were perfectly satisfied that a battle was to be fought on Drumossie, and that the Laird of Culdethel would be in it—though with whom the clans would fight, and for what, they could not pretend to tell.

Having finished our discussion on this singular second-sight sort of superstition, Wully Mackenzie struck up on his pipes. The pipes are the true instrument of the Highlands, as the harp is that of Wales, or the guitar of Spain. We never felt so strongly their power as on this occasion. Our musician was, as I have said, a short, stout Highlander. He was clad in coarse blue cloth, every thread of which his mother had spun, and which, when woven, had been made up too by his mother and sister in this very cabin; yet, as he stood playing his native airs, he seemed quite inspired, and we could not help being struck with the manliness of his attitude, and of his whole bearing. We never heard the music of the bagpipe in perfection till then. He played the tune with which the Highlanders were said to have marched into the battle of Culloden. We could see the gallant bands pass over the heath on which we were gazing through the open door. We could see the glimmer of their weapons, and the fluttering of their tartans, and feel, peaceful people as we are, the romantic spirit of heroism which had led them on their expedition into England, and now brought them here to destruction.

Our gallant piper never seemed weary of playing; and as it was a treat to sit in a Highland hut, and hear such a musician, we got him to play all the interesting airs that we could recollect. There scarcely was one that he was not master of; and on no occasion did we ever listen to music that so powerfully and variously affected us. He played pibrochs and marches, and, spite of our better judgments, we could not help kindling into the admiration of clan warfare; but the celebrated dirge, of which he related the origin, with which Highlanders march to the shore when they are about to embark as emigrants to some distant clime*—

Cha till, cha till, cha till, mi tuille.
We return, we return, we return no more !

—it was impossible to listen to it without tears.

* This is called Mackrimmon's Lament. Sir Walter Scott has written words to this air, and gives the following as the origin of it: " Mackrimmon, hereditary piper to the Laird of

Let no one despise the droning of the bagpipe that has not heard it as we heard it that day.

We took leave of this simple, intelligent, and kind-hearted family, and walked back, on a delicious evening, a nearer way over the fields to Inverness; having passed one of the pleasantest days of our life on the Field of Culloden.

Macleod, is said to have composed this lament when the clan was about to depart on a distant and dangerous expedition. The minstrel was impressed with a belief, which the event verified, that he was to be slain in the approaching feud, and hence the Gaelic words:—' *Cha till mi tuille ; ged thilles Macleod, cha till Mackrimmon.*' I shall never return ; although Macleod returns, yet Mackrimmon shall never return.''

Wully Mackenzie had a different version of the tradition. That there was a cave in the isle of Sky which had never been explored to any termination. That Mackrimmon and another bard, Macleod, dared each other to explore it; and that Mackrimmon composed this lament on the occasion, and went playing it into the cave, from which neither of the bards reappeared.

VISIT TO STRATFORD–ON–AVON, AND THE HAUNTS OF SHAKSPEARE.

THE country about Stratford is not romantic, but extremely pleasant. The town stands in a fine open valley. The Avon, a considerable stream, winds past it through pleasing meadows. The country is well cultivated, and the view of wooded uplands and more distant ranges of hills, gives spirit to the prospects. The town itself is a good, quiet, country town, of perhaps four or five thousand inhabitants. In Shakspeare's time it could be nothing more than a considerable village; for by the census of 1801 the total of its inhabitants was but 2418. In that day, the houses were, no doubt, built of wood or of framework, such as the dwelling of Shakspeare's parents still remains. Fires appear, by the history of the place, to have been frequent and destructive. In the 36th and 37th of Elizabeth two furious fires occurred, and so reduced the property of the inhabitants as to compel them to petition parliament for a remission of subsidies and taxes, and for a portion of £36,000, which had been granted for the relief of decayed cities and towns. The residence of Shakspeare himself narrowly escaped.

Stratford appears now to live on the fame of Shakspeare. You see the mementos of the great native poet wherever you turn. There is the Mulberry-tree Inn; the Imperial Shakspeare Hotel; the Sir John Falstaff; the Royal Shakspeare Theatre: the statue of Shakspeare meets your eye in its niche on the front of the Town-hall. Opposite to that, a large sign informs you that there is kept a collection of the relics of Shakspeare, and not far off you arrive at another sign, conspicuously projecting into the street, on which is proclaimed,— "IN THIS HOUSE THE IMMORTAL BARD WAS BORN." The people seem all alive to the honour of their town having produced Shakspeare. The tailor will descend from his shopboard, or the cobbler start up from his stall, and volunteer to guide you to the points connected with the history of the great poet. A poor shoemaker, on my asking at his door the nearest way to the church containing Shakspeare's tomb, immediately rose up and began to put on his coat. I said, "No, my friend, I do not want you to put yourself to that trouble; go on with your work—I only want you to say whether this way be the most direct." "Bless you, sir," said the man, taking up his hat, "I dont want any thing for showing a gentleman the way to Shakspeare's tomb; it is a pleasure to me. I am fond on't; and a walk, now and then, does me good." The old man bustled along, holding forth with enthusiasm in the praise of Shakspeare, and coming up to the sexton's house, and knocking,—"There," said he, "I have saved you ten minutes' walk :— don't forget to look at old Johnny Combe!" and was turning off highly pleased that he had done something to the honour of Shakspeare, and reluctant to receive even the value of a glass of ale for his services.

The Royal Shakspeare Club annually celebrate the birth of Shakspeare on the 23d of April, and even Washington Irving is held in great honour for having recorded in his Sketch-Book his visit to his tomb. At one of the inns they show you Washington Irving's room and his bed. In the Red Horse, at which I stayed, my room was adorned with his sole portrait, and all the keepers of Stratford albums take good care to point out to you the signature of Washington Irving, the American who spoke so highly of Shakspeare.

It is pleasing to find the prophet enjoying so much honour in his own country; and yet I shall have a fact or two presently to mention, which will

require the serious attention of the people of Stratford, if they do not mean all this show of zeal for
the poet's memory to appear empty and incon-
sistent.

One of the first places which I hastened to visit
was the birth-place of Shakspeare's wife; the
rustic cottage where he wooed, and whence he
married her. Millions, perhaps, have visited the
house where he was born; tens of thousands have
certainly inscribed their names on the walls of that
simple chamber where he is said to have first seen
the light; but not so many have visited, or known
of, or inquired after the house where his modest,
faithful, and affectionate wife,

Ann Hathaway, she hath a way,

was born, and lived, and became the wife of Shakspeare when he was nineteen, and she twenty-
seven.

Shakspeare seems to have had no personal ambition. If he had, we should have had more account of the incidents of his existence. He seems
to have thrown off his inimitable dramas, rich with
passion and poetry, more from the very enjoyment
of the act, than from the glory to be derived from
them. So, too, in his youth, he married the first

humble object of his affections; and after having seen all the fascinations of London life, after having conversed with the most celebrated beauties and wits of Elizabeth's splendid court, he retired with a competence to the quiet uneventful town of Stratford, the quiet haunts of his youth, and to domestic peace with his true Ann Hathaway.

There is nothing more wonderful in the character of Shakspeare than the perfect indifference shown to the fate of his inimitable dramas. For thirteen years after his retirement from the stage, and those years the very prime of his existence— for he died at the early age of fifty-two—he continued to live, and that in a great degree in the perfect leisure of Stratford, without apparently taking the slighest means to secure a correct edition of his works. He threw them off with the greatest imaginable ease and rapidity, the " Merry Wives of Windsor" being said only to have occupied a fortnight in the composition, and to have left them to the care of the public as stoically as the ostrich leaves its eggs to the sun. It could not be that he was insensible to their merit, for in his sonnets he gives us repeated assurances of the immortality of his muse; but it would seem as if, satisfied with the consciousness that he had done enough to secure his eternal fame, he followed his natural bent for the enjoyment of domestic life, and the entire forgetfulness of public concerns in which he was absorbed by it, testifying that there lay his entire happiness. That he spent the greater portion of the last sixteen years of his life at Stratford there is every reason to believe, having purchased for his residence one of the best houses of his native town, in 1597, which, having repaired and improved, he named New Place; nor is any other trace of him discoverable, independent of his literary exertions, from that year, except that in 1602 he was at Stratford, adding a new purchase of one hundred and seven acres of land to his former purchase of New Place. Not all the havoc committed by players and publishers on the sense and diction of his great dramas could rouse him from his domestic rest. "He made," says Johnson, " no collection of his works, nor desired to rescue those that had been already published from the depravations that obscured them, or to secure to the rest a better destiny by giving them to the world in their genuine state. . . . They were transcribed for the players by those who may be supposed to have seldom understood them; they were transmitted by copiers equally unskilful, who still multiplied errors; they were, perhaps, sometimes mutilated by actors, for the sake of shortening the speeches, and were, at best, printed without corrections of the press."

All this were enough to have roused, one would have thought, any author that had but sufficient ambition to write, but it disturbed not Shakspeare, and it must appear that the astonishing power displayed in his dramas was not the most wonderful quality of his nature. He had a mind that could not only achieve what was beyond the fame of other men, but a calm indifference even for his own fame, that more resembled the elevation of a divine nature than the nervous temperament of humanity. How different is this, even to the sensitiveness of his own youth, when the insult which he supposed himself to have received from Sir Thomas Lucy stung him to the quick, and induced him to gibbet him in ballads, and run for miles to fix them on his park-gate; an irritability so lasting that it revived and issued to the light again in the "Merry Wives of Windsor."

That Shakspeare valued the enjoyments of domestic life, beyond both the brilliant life of successful literature in London and beyond the fame of his works, his long quiet retirement at Stratford sufficiently proves. There have not been wanting those who have accused him of indifference or infidelity towards his wife; but, whatever might be

the occasional dissipations in which he might indulge during his London sojourn, he has himself
left the most triumphant testimonies of his strong
and changeless affection to his Ann Hathaway,*
and that it was in the depth of domestic existence
that he found his real happiness. Nothing can be
more beautiful than those of his sonnets which
refer to these subjects.

> Let me not to the marriage of true minds
> Admit impediments. *Love is not love*
> *That alters when it alteration finds,*
> *Or bends with the remover to remove.*
> *O no! it is an ever-fixed mark,*
> *That looks on tempests, and is never shaken.*
> It is the star of every wandering bark,

* The author of the beautiful and able romance of " The
Youth of Shakspeare" has, contrary to his usual sagacity,
and without any sufficient historic evidence, and contrary,
moreover, to the evidence of Shakspeare himself, here produced, unfortunately fallen into the former opinion, that of
his alienation from her whom the writer himself thus describes in Shakspeare's days of courtship:—" To him every
thing was Ann Hathaway, but especially all wisdom, good-
ness, beauty, and delight, took from her their existence, and
gave to her their qualities. She was, in brief, the sun round
which the rest of creation must needs take its course."—
Vol. ii. p. 183.

Whose worth's unknown, although his height be taken.
Love 's not Time's fool, though rosy lips and cheeks
Within his bending sickle's compass come ;
Love alters not with his brief hours and weeks,
But bears it out even to the edge of doom.
If this be error, and upon me proved,—
I never writ, nor no man ever loved.

There never were fourteen lines which so deeply and eternally express the sentiment clearly springing from the bottom of the poet's soul, of the unchangeableness of true affection. That one sonnet is enough to cast to the winds every malignant slander against the true heart of Shakspeare. That he, like other men, had fallen into errors, he was the first most earnestly and eloquently to avow; but where was the man, that after having won the fame that he had, and passed through the Circean enchantments of metropolitan beauty, and splendour, and wit as he had, ever gave so marvellous a proof that his heart of hearts was not in them, but that his only hope and idea of true happiness was in his native fields, and in the home of his wedded affection? What accuser could venture to stand up against such a man, after reading the very next sonnet, the continuation, in fact, of the former?

10*

Accuse me thus,—that I have scanted all,
Wherein I should your great deserts repay ;
Forgot upon your dearest love to call,
Whereto all bonds do tie me, day by day ;
That I have frequent been with unknown minds,
And given to time your own dear-purchased right ;
That I have hoisted sail to all the winds,
Which should transport me farthest from your sight.
Book both my wilfulness and errors down ;
And on joint proof surmise accumulate ;
Bring me within the level of your frown,
But shoot not at me in your wakened hate :
Since my appeal says, I did strive to prove
The constancy and virtue of your love.

That his long absence, for it does not appear
that his wife ever left Stratford to reside with him
in town, had occasioned some misunderstanding
and estrangement between her and himself, would
appear from several of his sonnets, which are the
only records which he has left of his life and internal feelings ; but the sorrow and repentance which
he expresses are more than enough to unbend the
brow of the sternest judge, much more of a tender
and loving wife.

O, never say that I was false of heart,
Though absence seemed my flame to qualify!

As easy might I from myself depart,
As from my soul which in thy heart doth lie.
That is my home of love: if I have ranged,
Like him that travels, I return again;
Just to the time, not with the time exchanged;
So that myself bring water for my stain.
Never believe, though in my nature reigned
All frailties that besiege all kinds of blood,
That it could so preposterously be stained,
To leave for nothing all thy sum of good:
For nothing this wide universe I call
Save thou my rose, in it thou art my all.

Alas! 'tis true I have gone here and there,
And made myself a motley to the view;
Gored mine own thoughts, sold cheap what is most dear,
Made old offences of affections new.
Most true it is that I have looked on truth
Askance and strangely; but, by all above,
These blenches gave my heart another youth,
And worst essays proved thee my best of love.
Now all is done, save what shall have no end:
Mine appetite I never more will grind
On newer proof to try an older friend,`
A god in love to whom I am confined.
Then give me welcome, next my heaven the best,
Even to thy pure, and most, most loving breast.

O for my sake do you with fortune chide,
The guilty goddess of my harmful deeds,
That did not better for my life provide,
Than public means, which public manners breeds.

Thence comes it that my name receives a brand,
And almost thence my nature is subdued
To what it works in, like the dyer's hand:
Pity me then, and wish I were renewed;
Whilst, like a willing patient, I will drink
Potions of eysell* 'gainst my strong infection,
No bitterness that I will bitter think,
No double penance to correct correction.
Pity me then, dear friend, and I assure ye
Even that your pity is enough to cure me.

In these sonnets we have not only the most touching confession of his errors, but some clue afforded to that neglect and contempt of his dramatic works which we have already noticed. He clearly regarded his profession of an actor as a degradation, as no doubt it was considered in the eye of those times. He probably regarded his dramas as mere compositions written to advance his fortune, and as standing testimonies to that mode of life which he regarded with aversion. This, it is probable, was the cause why he so entirely neglected them, and turned, as it were, his very thoughts from them, as reminding him of many things, during the period of their production, which he would fain forget for ever. The very next sonnet, and the only one which I shall here

* Vinegar.

indulge myself in transcribing, most strongly expresses this feeling, and the formation of that resolution to which he so inflexibly adhered to the day of his death.

> Your love and pity doth the impression fill,
> Which vulgar scandal stamped upon her brow:
> For what care I who calls me well or ill,
> So you o'ergreen my bad, my good allow?
> *You are my all-the-world*, and I must strive
> To know my shames and praises from your tongue;
> None else to me, nor I to none alive
> That my steeled sense, or changes, right or wrong.
> In so profound abysm I throw all care
> Of others' voices, that my adder's sense
> To critic, and to flatterer stopped are.
> Mark how with my neglect I do dispense:—
> You are so strongly in my purpose bred
> That all the world besides, methinks they are dead.

Impressed with the feelings and the history conveyed in these sonnets, I must confess that there was no spot connected with Shakspeare at Stratford that so strongly interested me as Shottry, the little rustic village where Ann Hathaway was born, and where Shakspeare wooed, and whence he married her. The house in which he was born is turned into a butcher's shop; his birth there was a mere accident, and the accidents of time have not

added to the intrinsic interest of the place: the
house which he built or improved for himself, and
in which he spent the last years of his life, was
pulled down, and dispersed piece-meal by the
the infamous parson Gastrell, who thus " doomed
himself to eternal fame" more thoroughly than the
fool who fired the Temple of Diana ; but the birth-
place and the marriage-place of Ann Hathaway, is
just as it was ; and, excepting the tombs of Shakspeare and herself, the only authentic and un-
changed traces of their existence here.   I therefore
hastened away to Shottry the very first moment
that I could get out of the inn.   It is but a short
walk to it across some pleasant meadows, and I
pleased myself with thinking as I strode along,
with what delight Shakspeare in his youth trod the
same path on his way to see his fair Ann Hathaway; and how often, in his latter years, when he
had renounced public life, and she was his " all-the-
world," they might, led by the sweet recollections
of the past, often stroll that way together, and perhaps visit some of their kindred under the same
rustic roof.

The village is a real rustic village indeed, consisting of a few farm-houses, and of half-timbered
cottages of the most primitive construction, standing apart, one from the other, in their old gardens

and orchards. Nothing can exceed the simplicity
and quiet of this rustic hamlet. It is the *beau ideal*
of Goldsmith's Auburn. The village public-house
is the " Shakspeare Tavern," a mere cottage like
the rest. No modern innovations, no improvements, seem to have come hither to disturb the
image of the past times. The cottages stand apart
from each other, in their gardens and orchard-
crofts, and are just what the poets delight to describe. The country around is pleasant, though
not very striking. Its great charm is its perfect
rurality. Ann Hathaway's cottage stands at the
father end of this scattered and secluded hamlet, at
the feet of pleasant uplands, and from its rustic
casements you catch glimpses of the fine breezy
ranges of the Ilmington and Meon hills, some miles
southward; and of Stratford church spire eastward
peeping over its trees.

The cottage is a long tenement of the most
primitive character; of timber framing, filled up
with brick and plaster-work. Its doors are gray
with age, and have the old-fashioned wooden
latches, with a bit of wood nailed on the outside of
the door to take hold of while you pull the string;
just such a latch as, no doubt, was on the door of
Little Red Riding-Hood's grandmother, when the

wolf said to the little girl, "pull the string, and you'll get in."

The antiquity of the house is testified by the heads of the wooden pins which fasten the framing, standing up some inches from the walls, according to the rude fashion of the age, never having been cut off. The end of the cottage comes to the village road; and the side which looks into the orchard is covered with vines and roses, and rosemary. The orchard is a spot all knolls and hollows, where you might imagine the poet, when he came here a-wooing, or in the after-days of his renown, when he came hither to see his wife's friends, and to indulge in day-dreams of the past, as he represents the king of Denmark

> ——Sleeping within mine orchard,
> My custom always of the afternoon——

lying on the mossy turf, and enjoying the pleasant sunshine, and the flickering shadows of the old apple-trees. The orchard extends up the slope a good way; then you come to the cottage garden, and then to another orchard. You walk up a little narrow path between hedges of box, and amongst long grass. All the homely herbs and flowers which grow about the real old-English cottage, and which Shakspeare delighted to introduce into his poetry—the rosemary, celandine, honeysuckle, marigold, mint, thyme, rue, sage, etc., meeting your eye as you proceed.

The commentators on Shakspeare have puzzled themselves wonderfully about some of the plainest matters of his text, and about none more than the identity of the dewberry. In the Midsummer Night's Dream, Titania tells the fairies to be kind to Bottom:

> Be kind and courteous to this gentleman;
> Hop in his walks, and gambol in his eyes;
> Feed him with apricocks and dewberries,
> With purple grapes, figs, and mulberries;
> The honey-bags steal from the humble-bees, etc.

These same dewberries have cost the expounders of his text a world of trouble. As apricots, grapes, and figs are very good things, they could not bring their fancies to believe that the fairies would feed Bottom on aught less dainty, even though he yearned hungrily after good oats and a bundle of hay. All kinds of fruits were run over in the scale of delicacies, and not finding any of the finer sorts which ever bore the name of dewberry, they at last sagely concluded that it must be a gooseberry, be-

cause the gooseberry is only once mentioned as a
gooseberry in all his dramas.   A wise conclusion!
What a pity that those laborious and ingenious
commentators would but step occasionally out of
their studies, and go into Shakspeare's own neighbourhood, and hear the peasantry there talk.   They
would not only have long ago discovered what a
dewberry is, but might hear many a phrase and
proverb, that would have thrown more light on the
text of Shakspeare, than will ever stream in through
a library window in half a century.   A dewberry
is a species of blackberry, but of a larger grain, of
a finer acid, and having upon it a purple bloom like
the violet plum.   It is a fruit well known by that
name to botanists (*rubus cæsius*), and by that name
it has always been well known by the common
people in the midland counties.   As I walked round
the orchard of Ann Hathaway, I was quite amused
to see it growing plentifully on the banks; and
taking up a sprig of it with some berries on it, I
asked almost every countryman and countrywoman
whom I met during the day, what they called that
fruit.   In every instance, they at once replied, " the
dewberry."   While I was in that neighbourhood I
repeatedly asked the peasantry if they knew such
a thing as a dewberry.   In every case they replied,
" To be sure, it is like a blackberry, only its grains

are larger, and it is more like a mulberry." A very
good description. "Yes," said others, "it grows
low on the banks; it grows plentifully all about this
country." So much for all the critical nonsense
about the dewberry.

I could not avoid noticing many such little
touches of natural imagery with which Shakspeare
has enriched the poetical portion of his text, as I
strolled about this garden and orchard. In the
Midsummer Night's Dream, Act iv., Shakspeare
says,

> The female ivy so
> Enrings the barky fingers of the elm.

Why the *barky* fingers of the elm? Because the
young shoots of the elm and those of the maple
cover themselves with a singular corky bark,
which rises in longitudinal ridges, of frequently
more than a quarter of an inch high, and presenting a very singular appearance. It is a curious
fact that the elm is the great natural growth of the
country about Stratford, and must have been particularly familiar to Shakspeare's eye, and in this
very orchard he must have seen plenty of the very
images he has used. I pleased myself with imagin-
ing the quiet happiness which he had enjoyed with

his Ann Hathaway in this very spot, while these
rural images and happy illustrations silently flowed
into his mind from the things around him.   There
was an old arbour of box, the trees of which had
grown high and wild, having a whole wilderness
of periwinkle at their feet; and upon the wooden
end of a shed forming one side of this arbour,
grew a honeysuckle, which seemed as though it
might have grown in the very days of Shakspeare,
for it had all the character of a very old tree; little
of it showing any life, and its bark hanging from
its stem in filaments of more than a foot long, like
the tatters and beard of an ancient beggar.   At the
door looking into this orchard is a sort of raised
platform up three or four steps with a seat upon it,
so that the cottagers might sit and enjoy at once
the breeze and the prospect of the orchard and
fields beyond.   There is a passage right through
the house, with a very old high-backed bench of
oak in it, said to have been there in Shakspeare's
time, and old enough to have been there long before.   The whole of the interior is equally simple
and rustic.   I have been more particular in speaking of this place, because perhaps at the very
moment I write these remarks this interesting
dwelling may be destroyed, and all that I have
been describing have given way to the ravages of

modern change. The place is sold, and perhaps the cottage of Ann Hathaway is now no more. A Mr. Barns, a farmer of the neighbouring hamlet of Luddington, has bought the whole property for 300*l.*, and talks of pulling down the house at spring. He has already pulled down some of the neighbouring cottages, and built up a row of red staring ones in their places; and already he has made an ominous gap into Ann Hathaway's orchard! The Taylors. the old proprietors, who have lived in the cottage for many years, were gone, the very morning I was there, to Stratford, to sign the conveyance.

PRESENT CONDITION OF THE SHAKSPEARE FAMILY.

As I went to Shottry, I met with a little incident which interested me greatly by its unexpectedness. As I was about to pass over a stile at the end of Stratford into the fields leading to that village, I saw the master of the national school mustering his scholars to their tasks. I stopped, being pleased

11*

with the look of the old man, and said, "You seem
to have a considerable number of lads here; shall
you raise another Shakspeare from amongst them,
think you?"   "Why," replied the master, "I have
a Shakspeare now in the school." I knew that
Shakspeare had no descendants beyond the second
generation, and I was not aware that there was
any of his family remaining. But it seems that
the posterity of his sister Joan Hart, who is mentioned in his will, yet exist, part under her marriage name of Hart, at Tewkesbury, and a family
in Stratford of the name of Smith.

"I have a Shakspeare here," said the master
with evident pride and pleasure. "Here, boys,
here!" He quickly marshalled his laddish troop
in a row, and said to me, "There now sir, can
you tell which is a Shakspeare?" I glanced my
eye along the line, and instantly fixing it on one
boy, said, "That is the Shakspeare." "You are
right," said the master; "that is the Shakspeare:
the Shakspeare cast of countenance is there. That
is William Shakspeare Smith, a lineal descendant
of the poet's sister."

The lad was a fine lad of, perhaps, ten years of
age; and certainly the resemblance to the bust of
Shakspeare, in the church at Stratford, is wonderful, considering he is not descended from Shak-

speare himself, but from his sister, and that the seventh in descent. What is odd enough, whether it be mere accident or not, that the colour of the lad's eyes, a light hazel, is the very same as that given to those of the Shakspeare bust, which it is well known was originally coloured, and of which exact copies remain.

I gave the boy sixpence, telling him I hoped he would make as great a man as his ancestor (the best term I could lay hold of for the relationship, though not the true one), or, at all events, a good man. The boy's eyes sparkled at the sight of the money, and the healthful joyous colour rushed into his cheeks; his fingers continued making acquaintance with so large a piece of money in his pocket, and the sensation created by so great an event in the school was evident. It sounded oddly enough, as I was passing along the street in the evening, to hear some of these same schoolboys say to one another, " That is the gentleman who gave Bill Shakspeare sixpence."

Which of all the host of admirers of Shakspeare, who has plenty of money, and does not know what to do with it, will think of giving that lad, one of the nearest living representatives of the great poet, a good education, and a fair chance to raise himself in the world? The boy's father is a poor man,

—if I be not fanciful, partaking somewhat of the Shakspeare physiognomy,* but who keeps a small shop, and ekes out his profits by making his house a " Tom-and-Jerry." He has other children, and complained of misfortune. He said that some years ago Sir Richard Phillips had been there, and promised to interest the public about him, but that he never heard any more of it. Of the man's merits, or demerits, I know nothing; I only know that in the place of Shakspeare's birth, and where the town is full of " signs" of his glory, and where Garrick made that pompous jubilee, hailing Shakspeare as a " demi-god," and calling him " the god of our idolatry," and where thousands and even millions flock to do homage to the shrine of this " demi-god," and pour out deluges of verse of the most extravagant and sentimental nature in the public albums; there, as is usual in such cases, the nearest of blood to the object of such vast enthusiasm are poor and despised: the flood of public admiration at its most towering height, in its most vehement current, never for a moment winds its course in the slightest degree to visit them with its

* Ireland, when, in 1793, making collections for his "Views on the Avon," was much struck with the likeness to this bust in Thomas Hart, one of this family, who then lived in Shakspeare's house.

refreshment, nor, of the thousands of pounds spent in the practice of this poetic devotion, does one bodle drop into their pockets.

Garrick, as I have observed, once

> called the world to worship on the banks
> Of Avon, famed in song.   Ah, pleasant proof
> That piety has still, in human hearts,
> Some place,—a spark or two not yet extinct.
> The mulberry-tree was hung with blooming wreaths;
> The mulberry-tree stood centre of the dance;
> The mulberry-tree was hymned with dulcet strains;
> And, from his touch-wood trunk, the mulberry-tree
> Supplied such relics as devotion holds
> Still sacred, and preserves with pious care.
> So 'twas a hallowed time: decorum reigned,
> And mirth without offence.   No few returned,
> Doubtless much edified, and all refreshed.
>
> COWPER's TASK, B. vi.

But it does not appear that Garrick and his fellow-worshippers troubled themselves at all about the descendants of the poet's sister. The object, in fact, seemed, at the moment, rather to worship Garrick even than Shakspeare. How then could any ray of sympathy diverge from two "demi-gods" to the humble relatives of one of them? And why should it? I hear learned utilitarians asking— why? What should lead the ragged descendants

of poets and philosophers to forsake self-depend-
ence and look to the admirers of their ancestors for
benefit? What a shocking thing if they should,
especially in a nation which ennobles whole lines
for ever, and grants immense estates in perpetuity
for the exploit of some man, who has won a battle
which better never had been fought! What! shall
such men, and shall whole troops of lawyers, who
have truckled to the government of the day, and
become the tools of despotism in a country dreaming that it is free—shall men who have merely piled
up heaps of coin, and purchased large tracks of
earth, by plodding in the city dens of gain, or
dodging on the Stock Exchange,—shall such men
be ennobled, and their line for ever, and shall the
men who have left a legacy of immortal mind to
their country, leave also to their families an exclusive poverty and neglect? Will our very philosophic utilitarians tell us why this should be?

It might also be whispered that it would not be
much more irrational to extend some of that enthusiasm and money, which is now wasted on empty
rooms and spurious musty relics, on at least trying
to benefit and raise in the scale of society, beings
who have the national honour to be relics and mementos of the person worshipped, as well as old
chairs, and whitewashed butchers' shops. Does it

never occur to the votaries of Shakspeare, that
these are the only sentient, conscious, and rational
things connected with his memory which can feel
a living sense of the honour conferred on him, and
possess a grateful knowledge that the mighty poet of
their house has not sung for them in vain, and that
they only in a world overshadowed with his glory
are not unsoothed by its visitings?* But the poetic
veneration of the public need not yet be reduced
to this severe trial—there are plenty of relics of
Shakspeare (so called) for them to wonder and
exclaim over.

* It appears from the town records and inscriptions in the
church, that the Hathaways were very respectable people at
Shottry for generations after Shakspeare's time; and that the
Smiths were amongst the principal people of the town. One,
cotemporary with Shakspeare, was three times mayor. Three
of them appear in inscriptions as benefactors to the town;
and others as witnesses and trustees, both in deeds executed
by Shakspeare, and also by his grandaughter Lady Barnard,
his last descendant; so that a family friendship was evidently
maintained to the last.

RELICS OF SHAKSPEARE IN STRATFORD.

In front of the Town-hall, in a niche, stands the full-length figure of Shakspeare, cast for the jubilee, and presented by Garrick to the corporation; at which time this Town hall, a new erection, was dedicated also by Garrick to the memory of Shakspeare. " The bard," to use the words of Wheller, the historian of Stratford, " is represented in a graceful attitude, as on his monument in Westminster Abbey, resting upon some volumes placed on a pedestal, ornamented with three busts, *viz.* Henry the Fifth, Richard the Third, and Queen Elizabeth. Upon a scroll, to which he points, are the following lines, judiciously selected from his own Midsummer Night's Dream :—

> The poet's eye in a fine frenzy rolling,
> Doth glance from heaven to earth, from earth to heaven,
> And as imagination bodies forth
> The forms of things unknown, the poet's pen
> Turns them to shapes ; and gives to airy nothing
> A local habitation and a name.

Upon the pedestal beneath, are these words from Hamlet :—

Take him for all in all,
We shall not look upon his like again.

Within the hall is a painting of Shakspeare, by Wilson, wherein he is represented sitting in an antique chair, and upon the ground lie several books and MSS., as North's Plutarch's Lives, Hollinshed's Chronicles, Cynthio's Novels, etc., being some of the authors which Shakspeare consulted.

Opposite to this Town-hall is a house occupied by a Mr. Reason, who has a sign in front of it, announcing that there is kept a collection of articles which were in the house where the poet was born, and remained there till Mary Homby, the mother of the present Mrs. Reason, was obliged to leave it on account of the proprietor raising the rent so much in consequence of the numerous visits to it. She at first gave ten, then twenty, then forty pounds a-year for it; but the tide of visiters increasing, the demand of the landlord still rose with it, till either the man outvalued the income, or the patience of Mary Homby gave way. She gave notice to quit the house, and another person immediately took it. A violent feud arose between the out-going and the in-coming exhibitor. Mary Homby, of course, stripped the house of every article that had been shown as Shakspeare's. But she did not stop there. She deliberately, or perhaps, as will appear probable, rather hastily, took a brush and a pail of whitewash, and washed over all the millions of inscribed names of adoring visiters on the walls! At one fell swoop, out went the illustrious signatures of kings, queens, princes, princesses, ambassadors, ambassadresses, lords, ladies, knights, poets, philosophers, statesmen, tragedians, comedians, bishops, lord chancellors, lord chief justices, privy counsellors, senators, and famous orators; all the sweet tribe of duchesses, countesses, baronesses, honourables, and dishonourables,—out went they altogether, with as little remorse as if death himself had been wielding the besom of destruction, instead of Mary Homby her whitewash brush!

Mary Homby, having executed this sublime extinction of so many dignities, marched out with a lofty sense of the vacuum she left behind, carrying away with her the Albums into the bargain. The new tenant on entering was struck with a speechless consternation! In " the immortal bard's" own words, all the precious relics had

> Vanished like the baseless fabric of a vision,
> And left not a wreck behind.

Nothing at all but four bare walls! What was to be done? It was still Shakspeare's birth-place —but it was a very naked one indeed,—all the imposing relics were gone, and a rival shop was set up with them! She looked upon herself as swindled. She had a higher rent to pay, with a diminished stock, and a formidable rival, and she accordingly raised a loud clamour in the ears of the landlord. The landlord began to bluster with Mary Hornby, and claimed the goods as heir-looms,—as part and parcel of the property; but the lawyers told him a different story. He then claimed the Albums, and commenced proceedings to recover them, but with no better success. Money was then offered for them, but money could not buy them; so it was absolutely necessary to commence a-new with blank walls and blank books. It was a melancholy coming down. Where was the chair called Shakspeare's chair, which had stood in a niche in the room, and the arms of which alone had been sold for twenty-three guineas? Where were those two fine old high-backed chairs which were *said* to be given to Shakspeare by the Earl of Southampton, with the Earl's coronet and supporters (animals having an odd look, between lions and men, with big heads) upon them? Where was the little chair of the

same kind, called Hamlet's chair—the son of Shakspeare, who died when twelve years old? Where
was that precious old lantern made of the glass
of the house where Shakspeare died? The bust
taken and coloured accurately from the bust in the
church? The portrait of a boy, with a curious
high-laced cap on his head and an embroidered
doublet, *called* John Hathaway, the brother of Ann
Hathaway? The painting said to be done by
Shakspeare's nephew, William Shakspeare Hart,
representing Shakspeare in the character of Petru-
chio? The cup, and the knotted walking-stick
made from the crab-tree under which he slept in
Bidford Fields?* Where the various pieces of
carving from his bedstead? That old basket-hilted

* Bidford is a village about six miles from Stratford, where
it is said in Shakspeare's time was a set of rustic topers who
were in the habit of challenging the residents of neighbouring places to drinking-matches, and that on one occasion
Shakspeare was amongst the young men of Stratford who
accepted such a challenge. That, on returning homewards
defeated, the Stratfordians lay down under a crab-tree still
standing by the road-side, about half a mile from Bidford,
where they slept from Saturday night till Monday morning,
when they were roused by workmen going to their labour.
Shakspeare was the last to wake; and when his companions
urged him to return and renew the contest, he exclaimed—
"No! I have enough. I have drank with

sword which *looked* as though it had lain buried for a century or two on the field of Edge-hill or Worcester, but which was, in fact, no such thing, but the veritable sword with which Shakspeare performed in Hamlet, and which the Prince Regent had wanted so much to buy in 1815, saying—" *he knew the family very well that gave it to Shakspeare?*" Where was that? Ay, and still more, where was that grand old piece of carving which used to be over the mantel-piece, coloured and gilt, and representing David fighting with Goliath between the adverse armies; and over their heads, on a flying label or garter, this inscription, *said*, and sufficiently testified by the splendour of the verse, to be written by " the immortal bard" himself?—

> Goliath comes with sword and spear,
>   And David with his sling;
> Although Goliath rage and swear,
>   Down David doth him bring.
>   SAMUEL 17th. An. Dom. 1606.*

> Piping *Pebworth*, dancing *Marston*,
> Haunted *Hilbro'*, Hungry *Grafton*,
> Dudging *Exhall*, Papist *Wicksford*,
> Beggarly *Broom*, and Drunken *Bidford*."

* This was there at the time of Ireland's visit.

12*

The iron box that held the poet's will; Shakspeare's bench; pieces of his mulberry-tree; the box given to him by the Prince of Castile; a piece of the very matchlock with which he shot the deer; the portraits of Sir John Bernard and his lady Elizabeth, the grandaughter of Shakspeare; the portrait of Charlotte Clopton in her trance; the pedigree, and the will—where were they all? Carried off by the indignant and vindictive Mary Homby, who was too selfish to pay more than 40l. a-year for the house in which so great a genius was born; for all the great names of all the illustrious people, from all quarters of the world, written by the blacklead pencils of every known manufactory, and all these precious relics to boot,—such a collection as was never yet seen on this side of Loretto.

But the ravages of this modern Goth and Vandal, Mary Homby, could not be entirely repaired—they might, however, be in some degree mitigated; and as the disconsolate successor ruminated on the means—lo! a most happy and inspired idea occurred to her. Mary Homby had been in a passion, and perhaps she had forgotten to put any size into her whitewash. A brush was instantly applied to the walls,—the hope became at once a certainty!—Mary Homby *had* omitted the size, and by gentle and continued friction of the brush, the millions of pencilled names once more appeared in all their original clearness! The relics were at once pronounced—humbug;—new Albums were opened, and the Shakspeare show-room was restored to its ancient value. In fact, this house, which was some years ago purchased of Joan Shakspeare's descendants, the Harts, with other property, for 250*l.*, is now said to be worth 2000*l.*

THE SHAKSPEARE ALBUMS.

AMONGST the innumerable signatures on the walls, the woman points you out that of Schiller as that of *the* Schiller, but it is written in Roman and not German hand. She also points out about a yard from the floor that of Edmund Kean, in a large hand, and tells you that he kneeled down to write it, saying,—" that as most people were ambitious to place their names as high as possible, he would place his low, and thus it would be the longer unencroached upon." It is now covered all over with a mob of names, and even written over and over. Indeed, the whole surface of the walls, from top to bottom, all round the room, nay, even the ceiling is covered thick with names upon names, which, if transcribed, would fill many large volumes.

There is nothing more curious than the signatures and the characteristic combinations of signatures which albums kept at such places present. I generally copy a few of the most striking as I turn them over; and here is a sample, from those in the albums both at the house where Shakspeare was born, and those formerly carried off thence by Mary Homby, and now at the house of her daughter, Mrs. Reason.

1813. March 5th.—John Howard Payne, New York.·'
      Aug. 13th.—Dr. Rees.
        Sep. 3rd.—Henry, Bishop of London.
            Lord Cowper.
            Mrs. Opie.
        Oct. 1st.—William Rathbone, Liverpool.
1815. July 27th.—Washington Irving.
      Aug. 17th.—George P. R. and
            Col. M'Mahon.
        26th.—William Duke of Clarence.
            Arthur, Duke of Wellington.
1816. Aug. 22nd.—Duke and Duchess of St. Albans, etc.
        28th.—Byron.
1821. Aug.   Mr. W. Stewart Rose.
           Mr. W. Lockhart.
           Sir Walter Scott, etc.

1821. Oct. 14th.—William Jerdan, Brompton, London.

> To Nature, sages in the earlier time—
> To Nature, men, even in each savage clime,
> Before revealed a God, all bowed the knee;
> Here where the High-Priest lived, oh be it mine
> To breathe one prayer, that fervent one be thine,
> And Shakspeare, next to Nature, given to thee.—W. J.

1827.   Prince Puckler Muskaw.

1829.   Duc de Chartres.

1831. April 22nd.—Helena, Grand Duchess of Russia.

                        Countess of Nesselrode.

                        Prince Gagarin, and suite.

1831   July 19th.—James Montgomery.

1832.   June 25th.—A. Sedgwick.

                        W. Whewell.

1835.   Sep. 18th.—Jane Porter.

                        N. P. Willis.

        Oct. 1st.—Countess Guiccioli.

                        Dr. Dionysius Lardner.

1836.   June 26th.—Prince of Orange.

                        Alexander, Prince of the Netherlands.

1837.   July 1st.—Edwin Forrest.

                        Catherine Norton Forrest.

1838.   Aug. 28th.—Countess of Blessington.

                        Comte d'Orsay.

        30th.—Charles Matthews.

                        E. Vestris.

After all, the church is the most interesting place in Stratford connected with Shakspeare, because

you have here proofs of him and his family con-
nexions beyond all question.   There is the well-
known bust of him in a niche close to the commu-
nion rail, on the north wall of the chancel, placed
on a cushion, holding a pen in his right hand, and
his left upon a scroll.   Above his head are his
arms, and on each side of them a small sitting
figure; one holding in his right hand a spade, the
other, whose eyes are closed, to indicate mourn-
ing, has one hand upon a skull, and in the other an
inverted torch.   Beneath the cushion is engraved
this distich:

JUDICIO PYLIUM, GENIO SOCRATUM, ARTE MARONEM,
TERRA TEGIT, POPULUS MŒRIT, OLYMPUS HABET.

And on a tablet underneath, these lines—

Stay, passenger, why goest thou by so fast!
Read if thou canst, whom envious death hath plast
Within this monument, Shakspeare, with whome
Quicke Nature dide; whose name doth deck ye tombe
Far more than coste; sicth all ytt he hath writt
Leaves living art but page to serve his witt.

    Obiit Ano. Doi. 1616, Ætatis 53. Die 23. Ap.

    This monument is said to have been raised very
soon after Shakspeare's death.   Wheeler thinks it

probable that it was erected by Dr. John Hall, his son-in-law and executor, or relations, at a time when his features were perfectly fresh in every one's memory, or, perhaps, with the assistance of an original picture, if any such ever existed. He adds, that some verses by Leonard Digges, a cotemporary of the poet, prove that it was here before 1623; that is, within seven years of his death. Sir William Dugdale, in his Diary, states the artist to have been Gerard Johnson, " a Hollander, a tombe-maker, who lived in St. Thomas's Apostells." It is undoubtedly the most authentic representation of him that we possess, and we have some additional argument for its resemblance to the original in its likeness to the print in the folio edition of his works printed in 1623, which Ben Jonson, in his verses under it, plainly asserts to be a great likeness. Yet, when we call to mind how little notice was attracted to this spot for years after Shakspeare's decease, and how easily satisfied are country people in a piece of monumental art, we cannot entertain too sanguine notions that we have a very characteristic representation of Shakspeare before us.

The head must fulfil and confirm all the faith of the phrenologists; it is a noble structure, but the remarkable gravity and massiness of the features do not answer to our notions of that soul of mirth, and whim, and passion, which must have shone through the outer veil of Shakspeare. The character is that of a sensible, grave, and benevolent man.

It is well known that the bust was originally painted to resemble life; that the eyes were light hazel; the hair and beard auburn. The dress consisted of a scarlet doublet, over which was a loose black gown, without sleeves; the lower part of the cushion before him was crimson, and the upper green, with gilt tassels. In 1748 this monument was carefully repaired, and the original colours of the bust restored, the expense being defrayed by the receipts of the acting of Othello at the old Town Hall, which were given by Mr. Ward, the manager, grandfather of Mrs. Siddons. In 1793 the bust and figures above it, together with the tomb of John a Combe, were, to correct the false taste of the erectors, by the perpetration of the worse taste of altering an original monument of so much consequence, painted white, at the request of Mr. Malone.

Below, and in front of the monument, we have, facing the communion-rail, a row of inscribed flags, covering the remains of himself, his wife Ann Hathaway, his daughter Susanna, and her husband, Dr. John Hall. We see the rude sculpture of that

characteristic and awful warning which he left to
be placed over his remains.

GOOD FREND FOR JESUS SAKE forbeare

TO DIGG T—E DUST ENCLOASED HERE

BLESE BE T—E Man $\frac{T}{y}$ spares T—E S STONES

AND CURST BE HE $\frac{T}{y}$ MOVES MY BONES.

That this hearty malediction was not unneces-
sary; that Shakspeare knew the freedoms that the
worthy churchwardens, in their ignorant authority,
were accustomed to use with the dead in his native
place, is strikingly proved by the disgraceful liberty
taken with the tomb of his daughter Susanna.   Besides her arms, Hall impaling Shakspeare, and the
following inscription still remaining :—Here lyeth
ye body of Susanna, wife to John Hall, gent., the
daughter of William Shakspeare, gent.   She de-
ceased ye 11th of July A. D. 1649, aged 66,—there
was originally this epitaph:

Witty above her sexe ; but that's not all ;
Wise to salvation was good Mistris Hall;
Something of Shakespere was in that, but this
Wholly of him with whom she's now in bliss.

Then passenger, ha'st ne're a teare,
  To weepe with her that wept with all?
That wept, yet set herselfe to chere
  Them up with comforts cordiall.
Her love shall live, her mercy spread,
When thou hast ne're a teare to shed.

These verses were long ago obliterated to make way for another inscription, carved *on the same stone*, for Richard Watts of Ryhm Clifford, a person in no way related to the Shakspeare family, and who, no doubt, was buried in the grave of Mrs. Hall. Thus it is probable that had not Shakspeare taken care of his bones in his lifetime, they would long ago have been dug up, and added to the enormous pile which used to lie in the charnel-house, and which was seen, so late as the year 1793, by Mr. Ireland.

After reading the Latin verses on the tomb of Ann Hathaway, we glance into the eastern corner, just by, and lo! the tomb of John a Combe, with his effigy stretched upon it. It is said that this man was a thorough-paced usurer. He resided at Welcome Lodge, and afterwards at the College; that is, a mansion so called, which, at the time that Stratford church was a collegiate church, was the residence of the chanting priests and choristers. This, after the dissolution by Henry VIII., was granted to the Earl of Warwick, afterwards Duke of Northumberland, and at his attainder by Queen Mary, was resumed by the crown; then let to Richard Coningsby, Esq., and finally sold to John Combe, Esq., who died there without family in 1614, two years before Shakspeare. It is said that, during Shakspeare's residence in the later years of his life at Stratford, John Combe and he were on very sociable terms, and Combe, presuming on Shakspeare's good nature and his own moneyed importance, frequently importuned the poet to write him an epitaph, which, to the old gentleman's vast indignation, he did thus :—

> Ten in the hundred lies here engraved,
> 'Tis a hundred to ten if his soul be saved.
> If any one asks who lies in this tomb—
> " Oho !" quoth the devil, " 'tis my John a Combe !"

As if to obviate the effect of the witty sarcasm of the inexorable poet, who would not give him any other passport to posterity than what he justly deserved, we find emblazoned not only on John a Combe's tomb, but on the gold-lettered tablets of the church, that he left by will, annually to be paid for ever : 1*l.* for two sermons to be preached in this church ; 6*l.* 13*s.* 4*d.* "to buy ten gowndes for ten poore people ;" and 100*l.* to be let out to fifteen poor tradesmen of the borough, from three years to three years, at the rate of 50*s.* per annum, which increase was to be distributed to the inmates of the almshouse,—adding upon his tomb in large letters, VIRTUS POST FUNERA VIVIT. But, spite of all this; spite of thus charging on his tomb only two and a half instead of ten per cent. ; spite of this emblazonment in marble and gold before the eyes of all churchgoers, the witty words of the poet, scattered only on the winds, not merely survive, but are in every body's heart and mouth all round Stratford, and will be till the day of doom.

This church stands pleasantly, between Stratford and the Avon, surrounded by trees, with a pleached avenue up to the porch door. The chancel is of beautiful architecture, which has lately been restored with great care. It also contains some grotesque and curious carving on the seats, which used to be occupied by the chanting priests, and now serve the clergy at visitations.

CHARLECOTE HOUSE.

No person who feels a lively interest in the history and haunts of Shakspeare, will think he has seen all that has drawn him to his native neighbourhood till he has seen Charlecote, the abode of that Sir Thomas Lucy who drove Shakpeare, for his deer stealing and his satirical sallies, from the obscurity of his original condition and calling, to London and universal fame. Charlecote lies on the banks of the Avon, about four miles from Stratford. It is a pleasant walk along a pleasant level road, through a country well shaded with large elms, and presenting on one hand rich meadows, and on the other as rich corn-lands. It was a fine autumn morning when I set off to walk there, and I pleased myself, as in going to Shottry, that I was treading the ground Shakspeare had trod many a time, and gazed on the same scenery, if not on the very identical objects. As I passed over the bridge, going out of the town, I said, " It was here that Shakspeare passed in his way to Charlecote, to affix those merry verses to Sir Thomas's park-gate,

13*

which so nettled the old knight; and on many another occasion paused to gaze up and down the
quiet-flowing Avon, as I do now." The woods of
Charlecote began to rise in view before me, and
presently the house itself, in front of them, stood
full in view, and made me exclaim, " Ay, there is
the very place still where Shakspeare encountered
the angry old knight in his hall." A foot-path led
me across a field into the park, and I found myself
at the entrance of a long avenue of limes, which
led towards the house, but not to it. It was terminated by a figure, which appeared to beckon to
you. As I advanced, I met a country lad; " So,"
I said, " this, I suppose, is where Shakspeare came
for some of Sir Thomas Lucy's deer? You have
heard of Shakspeare, I warrant you." " Yes," said
the lad, " often and often, and yonder he is upon a
deer that he took." " What Shakspeare?" "Yes,
sir, Shakspeare." I went on towards the image,
wondering at the oddity of taste which could induce the Lucys to place an image of Shakspeare
there, and with the deer too! When I came near,
behold it was a leaden statue of poor innocent
Diana. She was in the attitude of the Apollo Bel-
videre, having apparently just discharged an arrow
and watching its career, still holding aloft the bow-
hand, and grasping the centre of the bow. Close

to her side was the figure of a fallow deer; and the
simple country people had converted her into Shakspeare.   That this odd mistake did not rest with
the boy, I satisfied myself by asking every country
man and woman that I met in the neighbourhood
what that image was, and all answered, "Shakspeare on a deer."   I suppose that, as the knees of
the goddess are a little bent and the deer placed
close to her left side, they had got the notion that
it meant to represent Shakspeare riding away on
the deer that he had caught.   Even a Scotch travelling tea-merchant that I fell in with, told me the
same story.   I asked him whether he had ever been
at the statue and examined it.   He replied he had.
" And did you not observe," I asked, " that it was
a woman, with a woman's bosom, in a woman's
dress, and with a crescent on her brow ?"   " In
troth," said the man, " I didna' just notice that
noo."   So completely has the notion of its being
meant for Shakspeare taken hold of the people's
fancies, that they see nothing in it but Shakspeare,
spite of sex and dress ; and the Scotchman thought
the crescent on the brow of the image merely meant
that Shakspeare stole the deer by moonlight!

Charlecote-House stands pleasantly on the banks
of the Avon, where it makes a bend.   One side
looks down upon the river and towards Stratford ;

the opposite front looks into the old court, now a
garden, and in part of which stands a fine old
gate-house, which the present proprietor, George
Lucy, Esq. intends to restore, and fit up in accordant style. This front is entered by a porch, built
to admit Queen Elizabeth when she paid a visit to
Sir Thomas. The house was built by the Sir
Thomas of Shakspeare notoriety, but has been
much enlarged and embellished by the present
Mr. Lucy, who has built two noble rooms facing
the river,—a dining and drawing-room,—and furnished the whole with great taste.

The park is finely wooded with the natural
growth of this part of the country, elms of a large
size, and is nobly stocked with fallow deer. Mrs.
Lucy told me that it was a very common and per-
petually repeated mistake that it was from this park
that Shakspeare stole the deer, but that it was actually from the old park of Fulbrook on the War-
wick-road, where Fulbrook Castle formerly stood,
which ground is now disparked. This accords
with Mr. Ireland's statement. It was, however, in
this hall that he was tried.

The entrance hall, the scene of Shakspeare's
examination, is a fine room, with a grained oaken
roof, having been restored with admirable taste ;
and contains objects which cannot be looked on

without great interest. The family paintings are collected, and well disposed around it, with others connected with the history of the family.

On the ample mantel-piece are the large, old-fashioned initials of Sir Thomas Lucy, T. L. raised and gilt; and the date of the building of the hall, 1558. Upon this mantel-piece also stands a cast of the bust of Sir Thomas, taken from his monument in the church. There is also a painting of him, sitting at a table with his lady; in a black velvet dress with slashed sleeves, large bunches at the knees, of a zigzag pattern, in black-and-white stripes; light-coloured roses in his shoes, and with a ruff and cuffs of point lace. The portrait and bust bear a striking resemblance to each other; and though they do not give us any reason to suppose him such an imbecile as Shakspeare in his witty revenge has represented Justice Shallow, they have an air of formal conceit and self-sufficiency that accord wonderfully with our idea of the country knight who would look on the assault of his deer as a most heinous offence, and would be very likely to hold his dignity sorely insulted by the saucy son of a Stratford woolcomber, who had dared to affix a scandalous satire on his park-gate, and to make him ridiculous to all the country.

After all, what Sir Thomas did was just what

nine-tenths of the country gentlemen of that or this
day would have done in like case. He appears to
have dealt gently with the young man in the first
instance; and it was not until the ugly verses, of—

A parliament member, a justice of peace,
At home a poor scarecrow, at London an asse, etc.

were fixed on his gate by the vindictive pride of
the embryo poet, that he began to threaten him
with the serious visitation of the law. The only
singularity of the case is, that Sir Thomas had
stumbled on a great poet by the merest chance,
and that before either he or any body, even the
poet himself, knew that he were one, and thereby
roused him, as the Edinburgh Review roused
Byron, to a full consciousness and demonstration
of his hidden strength. Who can tell whether, had
it not been for the agency of Sir Thomas and the
Edinburgh Review, we might at this moment have
been possessed of the noble poems of Shakspeare
and of Byron? But, as the Scriptures say, "Offences must needs come, but woe unto those by
whom they *do* come." So the Review and Sir
Thomas have alike won a notoriety that they never
dreamed of, by starting a lion where they supposed
themselves pursuing a very different beast.

I have frequently heard it said that all which Shakspeare asserted of Sir Thomas Lucy was true, and that his descendants continued to this day pretty much the same, and always went by the name of Shallow. It is a luckless doom to fall under the bann of an irritated poet, and such a poet as Shakspeare. "The daggers which he spoke, though he used none," were sure to stick fast in the wounded name, and the vengeance which he took on the original offender, must descend, in some degree, to his posterity. There will never want that spice of malice in the popular mind which delights to believe all that common prejudice delights to promulgate in such cases, and I can conceive few greater curses falling on an innocent family, than the brand of folly thus fixed upon it by the withering sarcasm of indignant genius. Who does not shrink from the very idea of being born under such a stigma? Who could hope to bear up against it unscathed in the great race of life? Who can tell the blasting and deadening, and dwarfing influence of such an actual finger of bitter and burning scorn, held up against you and your children? When, therefore, I beheld the pleasant abode of the Lucys, and saw the evidences of taste and refinement about it, and heard what I did of the present family, I could not help feeling how awful is the clinging curse of an incensed poet, and how fearfully unjust he may become to whole generations of guiltless spirits, in the unrestrained indulgence of his revenge on its immediate object.

It was a high and sincere pleasure to me to find the present descendants of Sir Thomas Lucy the very reverse of all that Shakspeare would persuade us that he was. On all sides, and from all classes of people, I heard the most excellent character of them. They were described as amiable, intelligent; as of the most domestic habits, and as spending the chief portion of their time on their estate here. The poor spoke of them with affection for their kindness. I had not the pleasure to find Mr. Lucy at home; but the house itself bore everywhere the most unequivocal testimonies of his taste : and I have rarely met with a lady that interested me more by her agreeable manners, intelligence, and tone of mind, than Mrs. Lucy, a sister of Lady Willoughby de Broke, of Compton-Verney, in the same neighbourhood.

Mr. Lucy has enriched Charlecote-House with a select collection of paintings; and as the house, owing to the domestic habits of the family, is not commonly shown, it may be acceptable to some of my readers to have a passing mention of them.

In the hall, however, which we will mention first,

the pictures are, as I have said, chiefly family ones. Over the fire-place is a large family-piece—Sir Thomas, the grandson of old Sir Thomas, his lady, and six children, by Cornelius Janson, done while on a visit here. Sir Thomas has a mild contemplative look. His hair is of a sandy hue; his beard of the same colour, and peaked. The two youngest boys have also portraits as grown men in the hall, —Sir Fulke and Sir Richard Lucy.

There is a curious old view of the house and gardens in their original state; that is, in the state in which Shakspeare would see them. Captain Thomas Lucy and his lady, by Lely. This lady he left a widow, and she afterwards married the Duke of Northumberland.

In the library—portraits of Charles I. and II., Archbishop Laud, and Lord Strafford, by Henry Stone. Lord Herbert of Cherbury, by Isaac Oliver. A small, swarthy countenance, small dark and quick eyes, extremely black hair, and black mustachios, indicate in a lively manner the brisk and fiery spirit of this celebrated man. Here are also portraits of Henry VIII.; Rich, Earl of Holland; Marquess of Mantua, by Raffaelle; Sir Thomas Lucy again, in his youth; Isabelle, wife of the Emperor Charles V.; and the Lord Keeper Coventry. There are also in this room eight fine ebony chairs inlaid with ivory, two cabinets and a couch of the same, said to have been brought from Kenilworth, and to have been a present of Queen Elizabeth to Leicester.

In the drawing-room—Tenier's Wedding, painted by himself, purchased by the present Mr. Lucy for 1100*l.*, and for which he has refused 1300*l.* Cassandra delivered from captivity, by Guercino. Tempest, by Mole. Henry II. of France. Samson pulling down the temple, and Samson and the lion. Marketing parties going and returning, by Wouverman. Landscape by Cuyp. St. Cecilia, by Domenichino. Landscape, by Hobbima. Ditto, by Berghem, 1619. Interior of a room, by Peter de Hogh. Madonna and child, by Vandyke. Watermill and cattle, by Paul Potter. Here are also busts, by Behnes, of the present Mr. and Mrs. Lucy; and a splendid gold cup made for George IV., richly studded with jewels.

In the dining-room—Battle of a cock and turkey, by Ulnoebocker. Still-life,—cock and gardener, by Jacob Jordans. An arrest, by Peter Valentine. Woman spinning, said to be by Raffaelle in his early style. Horses, by Wouverman.

In Mrs. Lucy's morning-room there are a few good paintings. St. Catherine and a Magdalene. Christ's head, by Carradocio. But the most beau-

tiful thing, and one of the most beautiful in the
whole house, is the portrait of a female holding a
cup in one hand, with the other placed upon it—
her beautiful face full of a melancholy sentiment,
with rich golden locks hanging on her shoulders.
The subject and the artist are alike unknown. Mrs.
Lucy found it in the house, and had it cleaned ;
and it certainly is one of the most divine things
ever seen. The beauty of the whole countenance
—the fine large eyes full of thought and sorrow—
the high rich forehead—the glorious head, and the
pure and deep sentiment of the whole, mark the
hand of the master, and are worthy of Raffaelle
himself.   It is a being radiant with youth and
beauty, and rendered irresistibly attractive by the
soul and the sublime sorrow breathed through and
breathing from it.   Mrs. Lucy was inclined to believe it a Niobe, but to my feeling it could be
nothing else but one of the noble women who minis-
tered to our Saviour—a Mary, a Magdalene, or
the penitent and nameless woman who " washed
his feet with her tears, and wiped them with the
hairs of her head."*   Such a being, in the sublimity

* The old painters make Mary Magdalene this woman, but
there is no evidence of it in the Gospels.   Three of the evan-
gelists declare that this anointing took place at Bethany, and

of her grief, so far beyond any subject of the Gre-
cian mythology, inasmuch as the grief of any natural bereavement, however agonizing, falls short in
its solemn grandeur of that profound sorrow and
shame which surprise and overwhelm a noble soul
when it becomes aware of the original purity of
beauty which once was its own, and how much
" its inner self it has abused,"—can only be con-
ceived and expressed by a spirit of a similar elevation.   These circumstances point out this beautiful
female as belonging to the Gospel history, and to
the pencil of a great master.

   At a short distance, in the park, stands the little
church of Charlecote ; and it is well worthy of a
visit from the stranger.   It contains the monuments
of the Lucys, and they are some of the richest and
most beautifully executed to be found in any of our
country churches.   There, too, you see the hatchments of the different knights, with their *lucies* (the
three fishes—pikes) in the escutcheon, made so
notorious by Shakspeare. ˙Old Sir Thomas lies on
his tomb in effigy, and his lady by his side.   It is
from this effigy that the bust in the hall has been

John says it was by Mary the sister of Martha.   The others
do not name the woman ; and Luke says it occurred at Nain.

taken, with its ruff, and peaked beard cut square at the end.

If Sir Thomas has been pretty well misrepresented by the waggish wit of Shakspeare,* we must believe that his lady has not been the less so by the fragment of a ballad which has been preserved by Professor Barnes, taken down as an old woman sung it at an inn at Stratford, and attributed to Shakspeare, in which she is described as a most unfaithful wife. If any faith is to be put in the epitaph engraved on this tomb, which was written by Sir Thomas himself—" as by him that did best know what hath been written to be true," —she must have been, on the contrary, a very exemplary woman: " a woman," he says, " so garnished with virtue as not to be bettered, and hardly to be equalled by any." The tradition is, that she

---

* John Fox, the martyrologist, was received by Sir Thomas at the time when he was obliged to fly for his life on account of his religion, in Mary's reign, and was deserted by every one besides. It is said that Sir Thomas took care to have a good equivalent for his protection, by making Fox the tutor to his children, and that when that end was served, he dismissed him with little ceremony, and no care for his future provision. Admitting all this, it is evident still, that Sir Thomas gave him that shelter at a critical time, which no one else would give, and in so far was before his age.

went by the name of " the good Lady Lucy," and Newton in his " Memoirs of Pious Women," gives her an extraordinary character for virtue and benevolence.

Sir Thomas's son and successor, who appears to have only survived him five years, lies in his stately tomb by himself. His lady, in a black hood, is placed in a praying attitude in front of the tomb, thereby indicating that she was the sorrowful survivor; while, on the plinth, is a whole procession of little images of sons and daughters, two by two. Six sons on the panel before the mother, and eight daughters on that behind her. The tomb of the third Sir Thomas, the grandson of *the* Sir Thomas, and his lady, is a very splendid one by Bernini, executed in Italy. It is a pediment of white marble, bearing the family escutcheon, the panels and shafts of the columns black. It is indeed of beautiful workmanship. Sir Thomas is in a recumbent position, leaning on his elbow, as if contemplating the effigy of his wife, whose figure and drapery are finely wrought. Behind him, on the one hand, are seen books as in a library, with various classical titles on the back; and on the other hand, himself, mounted on his favourite horse—probably intended to intimate his prevailing tastes, as well as an accident in hunting which hastened his death. The bust of the lady is particularly soft and rich, the arms and hands are beautiful.

CLOPTON HALL.

THERE is one more place, the history of whose proprietors is, in a slight degree, connected with that of Shakspeare in this neighbourhood, which we will take some notice of before we quit his Stratford haunts altogether ; and the more because it is a specimen of a large class of old mansions which once held families of great note, but are now passed into other hands, leaving no trace of their once important inhabitants, beyond the monuments in the parish church; the brief record of their genealogy in the history of the county; and some fragments of mysterious traditions that float about amongst the common people, but which are fast fading away too.

The ground on which Shakspeare's own house in Stratford stood, had been the property of the Cloptons of Clopton. In course of time it was again purchased by a member of the Clopton family; and in 1742, Sir Hugh Clopton entertained Garrick, Macklin, and Dr. Delany there, under the poet's mulberry-tree. Shakspeare also mentions in his will, lands belonging to him in Welcome; which probably also had been the property of the Cloptons, as Welcome adjoins the present estate of Clopton, both of which are, in fact, now in the hands of one proprietor. At Welcome too, Shakspeare used to visit and make merry with his friends, John and William Combe.

But we have only to enter Stratford church to see that the Cloptons were the great family of that neighbourhood. At the east end of the north aisle, the chapel formerly dedicated to the blessed Virgin is occupied with their stately tombs. Above hang numerous hatchments, recording so many deaths, and family banners, dusty and worn with age, waved there too. These are now gone; but the monuments remain, with a massy and time-worn splendour which dwarfs all others around, and marks the once high estate of the race. Under a Gothic arch is raised an altar-tomb, about four feet and a half from the pavement, with numerous panels, originally filled with brazen shields of arms, but which have been long since torn away. A marble slab, without effigy or inscription, covers the tomb; but the arms of Clopton, with those of the city of London, and those of the company of woolstaplers, of which he was a member, carved and yet remaining on the arch above, mark it as the tomb of Sir Hugh Clopton, who in 1492 was Lord Mayor of London, and by his will directed that his remains should repose exactly on this spot. Sir Hugh, a younger branch of the ancient family of the Cloptons, had not disdained to enter into trade, and becoming not only very wealthy but Lord Mayor of London, was a man of a princely liberality. Besides numerous benefactions to the city of London, to Aylesbury, and other places, in building bridges and making causeways, leaving perpetual charity to the poor, etc.—he, at his own charge, built the Chapel of the Holy Trinity in Stratford, the transept of the church, and the bridge over the Avon; as is still recorded on a tablet on the bridge itself. Sir Hugh also left an exhibition to three poor scholars in Oxford, and three in Cambridge.

Besides the monument of this magnificent old Sir Hugh, the most conspicuous is that of George Carew, Earl of Totnes and Baron of Clopton. This is the Lord Carew who, when President of Munster under Queen Elizabeth, wrote the chronicle of the events in Ireland during the three years of his government, called by him *Hibernia Pacata*, and

published by his secretary and natural son, Sir
Thomas Stafford. He was the friend of Camden
the antiquary. He and his brother Richard Carew,
were his fellow collegians at Christ Church, Oxford,
and Camden styles him " a most affectionate lover
of venerable antiquity." Lord Carew became Baron of Clopton by marrying Joyce the sole heiress
of the family. The effigies of himself and countess
in alabaster, coloured to the life, lie under a large
ornamented arch, supported by Corinthian columns,
and adorned as well with numerous figures of
angels and cherubims, as with the various arms,
warlike accoutrements and insignia of his office of
master of the ordinance, carved in bas-relief. The
hearty old Earl, who has a most frank and goodly
aspect and bearing, is represented in armour; over
which is his mantle of estate, a coronet on his head,
and a lion couchant at his feet. If ever the outward form and visage bespoke the inner man, we
should say they did in this worthy nobleman. That
the effigy is a strong likeness of the living man is
testified by his existing portraits—and the likeness
is that of a right worthy nobleman; and Joyce
Clopton his countess must have been a fitting match
in generous and good disposition. Sir Thomas
Stafford, the natural son of the Earl, so far from
being a cause of unhappiness between this amiable

pair, was the attached friend of both; and as is recorded on a panel of this monument, not only lived long with them in affection, but desired to be buried near them, and is accordingly buried here with them. This is a pleasant record to be found on a tomb; but it is not the only one which shows the amiable heart of the countess. Another inscription tells, that here too lies buried " Mistres Amy Smith, sixty years of age and a maid, who for forty years had been the waiting gentlewoman of the Right Honorable Joyce, Ladie Carew, Countess of Totnes, and desired to be buried in the same church where her ladie intended to be buried." And accordingly on her death, at Nonsuch in Surrey, Lady Carew had her remains deposited here, "in gratefull memorie of her whom she had foun so good a servant." Far and wide might we look for another tomb bearing such beautiful records of the faith and affections of the good old times. The worthy Earl not only continued in high esteem with Elizabeth, but under James and Charles, by the latter of whom he was created Earl of Totnes; and, as if the calm sunshine of virtue and friendship had shed a sanative power upon their lives, all of these parties lived to an old age, the Earl himself being seventy-three and the Countess seventy-eight.

The stately old mansion where this family resided for more than five hundred years, stands advantageously on a fine upland about a mile above the town of Stratford, and commands all the fair vale in which Stratford stands. It looks full upon the woody spot to the right of the town in which Shottry lies nestled, and has for the boundary of its view, at the distance of some eight or ten miles, the long line of the Ilmington and Meon hills. Though thus elevated, it stands in a little hollow, as it were, in the upland slope, as if to give it that snug and protected air of which our ancestors were so fond, while behind it still ascend upland pastures, their hedgerows finely scattered with noble elms.

It was of this goodly old abode that a fair lady thus wrote to me on seeing the announcement of this volume. "I wonder if you know Clopton Hall, about a mile from Stratford-on-Avon. Will you allow me to tell you of a very happy day I once spent there. I was at school in the neighbourhood, and one of my schoolfellows was the daughter of a Mr. W——, who then lived at Clopton. Mrs. W—— asked a party of the girls to go and spend a long afternoon, and we set off one beautiful autumn day, full of delight and wonder respecting the place we were going to see. We passed through desolate, half-cultivated fields, till we came within sight of the house—a large, heavy, compact, square brick building, of that deep, dead red almost approaching to purple. In front was a large formal court, with the massy pillars sur-mounted with two grim monsters; but the walls of the court were broken down, and the grass grew as rank and wild within the enclosure as in the raised avenue walk down which we had come. The flowers were tangled with nettles, and it was only as we approached the house that we saw the single yellow rose and the Austrian briar trained into something like order round the deep-set dia-mond-paned windows. We trooped into the hall, with its tessellated marble floor, hung round with strange portraits of people who had been in their graves two hundred years at least; yet the colours were so fresh, and in some instances they were so life-like, that looking merely at the faces, I almost fancied the originals might be sitting in the parlour beyond. More completely to carry us back, as it were, to the days of the civil wars, there was a sort of military map hung up, well finished with pen and ink, showing the stations of the respective armies, and with old-fashioned writing beneath, the names of the principal towns, setting forth the strength of the garrison, etc. In this hall we were

met by our kind hostess, and told we might ramble
where we liked, in the house or out of the house,
taking care to be in the " recessed parlour" by tea-
time.   I preferred to wander up the wide shelving
oak staircase, with its massy balustrade all crumbling and worm-eaten. The family then residing at
the hall did not occupy one-half,—no, not one-third
of the rooms ; and the old-fashioned furniture was
undisturbed in the greater part of them.   In one of
the bed-rooms (said to be haunted), and which, with
its close pent-up atmosphere and the long shadows
of evening creeping on, gave me an 'eirie' feeling,
hung a portrait so singularly beautiful! a sweet-
looking girl with paly gold hair combed back from
her forehead, and falling in wavy ringlets on her
neck, and with eyes that ' looked like violets filled
with dew,' for there was the glittering of unshed
tears before their dark blue—and that was the likeness of Charlotte Clopton, about whom there was
so fearful a legend told at Stratford church. In the
time of some epidemic, the sweating-sickness, or
the plague, this young girl had sickened, and to all
appearance died. She was buried with fearful
haste in the vaults of Clopton chapel, attached to
Stratford church, but the sickness was not stayed.
In a few days another of the Cloptons died, and
him they bore to the ancestral vault ; but as they

descended the gloomy stairs, they saw by the torch-light, Charlotte Clopton in her grave-clothes leaning against the wall; and when they looked nearer, she was indeed dead, but not before, in the agonies of despair and hunger, she had bitten a piece from her white round shoulder! Of course, she had *walked* ever since. This was " Charlotte's chamber," and beyond Charlotte's chamber was a state-chamber carpeted with the dust of many years, and darkened by the creepers which had covered up the windows, and even forced themselves in luxuriant daring through the broken panes. Beyond, again, there was an old Catholic chapel, with a chaplain's room, which had been walled up and forgotten till within the last few years. I went in on my hands and knees, for the entrance was very low. I recollect little in the chapel; but in the chaplain's room were old, and I should think rare editions of many books, mostly folios. A large yellow-paper copy of Dryden's " All for Love, or the World Well Lost," date 1686, caught my eye, and is the only one I particularly remember. Every here and there, as I wandered, I came upon a fresh branch of a staircase, and so numerous were the crooked, half-lighted passages, that I wondered if I could find my way back again. There was a curious carved old chest in one of these passages,

and with girlish curiosity I tried to open it ; but the
lid was too heavy till I persuaded one of my companions to help me, and when it was opened, what
do you think we saw—BONES!—but whether human,
whether the remains of the lost bride, we did not
stay to see, but ran off in partly feigned, and partly
real terror.

" The last of these deserted rooms that I remember, the last, the most deserted, and the saddest,
was the Nursery,—a nursery without children,
without singing voices, without merry chiming
footsteps! A nursery hung round with its once
inhabitants, bold, gallant boys, and fair, arch-look-
ing girls, and one or two nurses, with round, fat
babies in their arms. Who were they all ? What
was their lot in life ? Sunshine, or storm? or had
they been ' loved by the gods, and died young ?'
The very echoes knew not. Behind the house, in
a hollow now wild, damp, and overgrown with
elder-bushes, was a well called Margaret's Well,
for there had a maiden of the house of that name
drowned herself.

" I tried to obtain any information I could as to
the family of Clopton of Clopton. They had been
decaying ever since the civil wars; had for a generation or two been unable to live in the old house
of their fathers, but had toiled in London, or

abroad, for a livelihood; and the last of the old
family, a bachelor, eccentric, miserly, old, and of
most filthy habits, if report said true, had died at
Clopton Hall but a few months before, a sort of
boarder in Mr. W——'s family. He was buried
in the gorgeous chapel of the Cloptons in Stratford
church, where you see the banners waving, and
the armour hung over one or two splendid monuments. Mr. W—— had been the old man's solici-
tor, and completely in his confidence, and to him
he left the estate, encumbered and in bad condition.
A year or two afterwards, the heir-at-law, a very
distant relation living in Ireland, claimed and ob-
tained the estate, on the plea of undue influence,
if not forgery, on Mr. W——'s part; and the last I
heard of our kind entertainers on that day, was
that they were outlawed, and living at Brussels."

After reading this account, I was strongly drawn
towards Clopton, and on my visit to Stratford, I
hastened eagerly to see a spot so attractive by its
history, and so graphically described. It was too
late. A new lord was in possession. After passing
through several hands from the period alluded to by
my fair correspondent, and through many dismal
stages of neglect and decay, Mr. Ward, the proprietor of Welcome, had purchased, and had had
sixty workmen for at least six months employed

15*

upon it. Those old staircases were now painted and polished into new ones. Those old oak floors had given way to new deal ones. Wagon-loads of lumber, as the new proprietor called it, wainscot, old chests and benches, and things of the past were carried away, and splendid stoves, and massy mantel-pieces of Italian marble, had succeeded the stern wide old-English fire-places. Modern furniture was standing about in confused heaps in the rooms; and fresh paintings of a higher character than the Cloptons ever knew, were in the act of ascending those walls where the grim Clopton portraits had hung so long; but which, such as still remained, were now consigned to a back gallery. " They are wretched affairs," said the young and gay lord of the house. " I am not at all related to the family; and I do not know what I could better do with them."

Perhaps nothing more could be expected. They clearly belonged to an era and a race that were gone by. They were things which had outlasted their legitimate masters :—

Another race had been, and other palms were won.

But I looked them over. They did not exceed two dozen in number, and amongst them I looked in vain for Charlotte Clopton, with " her locks of paly gold," or for Margaret, with " her beautiful face, and dark, brown ringlets flowing on her shoulders." " Was there not such and such a tradition?" I asked. " And such and such a picture? Margaret as a child with her little dog in her arms, and again in the bloom of maiden beauty?" " There were such traditions," it was carelessly replied, and in a tone which showed that there was no strong interest felt in such traditions. Youth, wealth, and fresh possession, and the eager novelty of fitting up a new abode were not calculated to generate a sentimental mood; and yet methinks the fate and the pictures of the past race of such an abode would have excited in my mind an interest, not the most trivial, amongst those feelings which give value to the possession.

Well, but where were the pictures of Charlotte and Margaret Clopton? They were not there! In some of the many changes which had occurred, somebody had taken them away—somebody, it is to be hoped, who valued them.

It was useless pressing further inquiries upon the new proprietor—but I saw some women collecting apples in the orchard, who were old enough to have known the house well in its former state. I asked them, and they knew the portraits familiarly,

just as described by my fair correspondent, and
they knew that they were there not very long ago.
One of them also went and showed me the spring
in which Margaret was drowned. In a woody
glade which runs up behind the house is a succession of fish-ponds, now half empty of water, and
neglected ; and beyond these, under the shade of
large elms, is the spring in which Margaret
drowned herself. It is a tank of perhaps three
yards long, and two wide, and of a considerable
depth, now arched over nearly level with the
ground, and only open at one end. The water
was so transparent that every part of the tank is
seen to the bottom, and a fearful and gloomy place
it is for any human creature to plunge into. What
must have been the misery and despair which must
have goaded Margaret's spirit in this old and solitary place, before she could venture to plunge in
there !

On a stone laid behind the spring, but which is
said to have been laid at its mouth, are inscribed
the initials S. I. C. 1686. No doubt those of Sir
John Clopton, who died in 1692, and who most
probably first enclosed this well. But who were
Charlotte and Margaret Clopton? Whose daughters were they? At what period did they live?
What more is known of the tragic death of Char-

lotte? What is known of the history, or the cause
of the suicide of Margaret? These are questions
that we ask of the local historian: but we ask in
vain. The facts to which they relate are such as
antiquaries, while hunting after genealogies, knights
and warriors, and heads of families, have too much
passed over, to the great loss of our domestic history. The dry outlines of family descent have been
scrupulously preserved, but the most touching and
characteristic passages in the home events of those
families themselves have been passed over as not
belonging to the province of topographer. What
would we not now give to recall them? What
would we not give, as we pass through the galleries of our ancient houses, or stand by family
tombs, and see the portraits or read the names of
numbers of whom no special record is left, to be
able to summon them before us, and hear what
befel them in their day? Even Dugdale, who,
unlike the general race of topographers, has rescued
so many of these fleeting traditions in his beloved
county of Warwick, has left no glimpse of the history of Charlotte or Margaret Clopton. Yet there
is no doubt but that the popular traditions respecting them are founded in fact. To the portraits of
these ladies, which were in the hall at the time of
the visit of my fair correspondent, and were well

known to the women with whom I conversed in
Clopton orchard, these stories were always attached. In Mr. Reason's collection of Shakspeare
relics, already mentioned, there is a painting of
Charlotte in her Trance; a lovely young woman
leaning back in a cushioned chair as in a profound
sleep, which, no doubt, was one of the family-pieces
of the hall. Every body thereabout was familiar
with just as much of Charlotte's history as is given
above by my fair friend; and the women in the
orchard said that Margaret had drowned herself in
the well called after her, on account of the death of
her lover in the civil wars. Who would not give
up the catalogue of a score of bearded knights,
grim Sir Johns and Sir Thomases, with all their
dates of birth and death, for the simple history of
these unfortunate damsels, which the historians of
the time did not deem worthy of their notice! We
may now inquire for them in vain.

Clopton, independent of its family interest, has,
in fact, little interest. It has no claims to fine
architecture or to value from works of art; but it
attracts our imagination as a specimen of those
mansions of old families which once were of importance, but are now, like their ancient proprietors, gone to decay, or are, as it were, resusci-
tated by the wealth of a modern purchaser. The

north and west sides of the house are said to have
been built in Henry VII.'s time; the south and east
part in that of Charles II. When Ireland visited it
in 1792 or 1793, he found in it a bed given to Sir
Hugh Clopton by Henry VII,, and in which he is
said to have frequently slept; the furniture being of
fine cloth of a darkish brown, with a rich fringe of
silk about six inches deep. In the attic story also
was a chapel, with scriptural inscriptions in black
letter, and religious paintings on the walls, as ancient as the house. In one place was a large fish,
with a hand at a distance dragging it forward with
a string; in others, scraps of poetry, such as these
lines:

> Whether you rise yearlye,
> Or goe to bed late,
> Remember Christ Jesus
> That died ffor your sake.

This chapel, which one of the Cloptons, a stanch
Catholic, is said to have used after the Reformation, is exactly such a chapel as is still found in the
roof of Compton-Winyates.* Mr. Ireland's son, the
fabricator of the Shakspeare MSS., in his " Confes-
sions" of that curious transaction, also states that

---

* See Visit to Compton-Winyates.

he was with his father on this visit, and saw "numbers of chambers in this antique mansion darkened
to obviate the expense of the tax on window-lights;
and in the cock-loft were piles of mouldering furniture of the age of Henry VII.; amongst the rest an
emblazoned representation of Elizabeth the Queen
of Henry VII., as she lay in state in the chapel
of the Tower of London, after having died in
childbed; which curious relic the then owner of
Clopton gave to Mr. S. Ireland, as a *picture* which
was in his opinion of no service, because, being on
vellum it would not do *to light the fire.*"

Mr. Ireland had been informed that many papers
had been removed from Shakspeare's house in
Stratford at the time of the fire, to this house; and
on inquiring if any such had ever been seen, the
proprietor made this answer, "By G—d, I wish
you had arrived a little sooner! Why, it isn't a
fortnight since I destroyed several basketfuls of
letters and papers, in order to clear a chamber for
some young partridges which I wish to bring up
alive; and as to Shakspeare, why there were many
bundles with his name wrote upon them. Why, it
was in this very fire-place I made a roaring bonfire
of them."

Mr. Ireland listened to this relation with feelings
not to be described, and starting from his chair,

exclaimed, "My God! sir, you are not aware of the loss which the world has sustained. Would to heaven I had arrived sooner!" Williams, the then proprietor, called his wife, who made the same statement, and lanterns were lighted, and the dark rooms of the house examined, but nothing further of the kind found. How far this story is true, considering the fabulating character of the younger Ireland, may be left to the faith of the reader, especially as the father, in his account of his visit, is silent on so remarkable a circumstance.

In its later years Clopton must have been, in its desolation, just the place for generating tales of superstition. Its old carving and decayed paintings, its ruinous windows and rotting floors,—all around its fences and gates going to decay, and its mighty trees spreading higher and wider, and casting over it a brooding gloom. It will now, no doubt, soon become a goodly and splendidly-furnished mansion; but the visible traces of the ill-fated Cloptons are nearly erased, and it can only in future be said, such a family once lived there, and such were the traditions of their fate. Amongst the portraits, that of Lord Carew, already mentioned, who married Joyce, the heiress of this house, was still to be seen, bearing a striking resemblance, both in form and feature, to the effigy in the church.

There were also one or two besides who exhibited lively and attractive features, but they are not by eminent masters, and therefore cannot claim a merit apart from their own identical importance, which has expired. The Cloptons have evidently been not only a powerful but a well-featured race; but they had not their poet, they had not even their painter, who could invest them with immortality. They, therefore, now hang in the back passage of a house no longer theirs. Its master does not share their blood; he has no interest in them, and how long they will be tolerated, even there, is a dubious problem.

Can any termination of the career of a once honoured and fortunate race, be imagined more melancholy? Yet, of how many a proud line is this the end!

As I returned towards Stratford, I met the new lady of the mansion driving up in her gay equipage, and I could not help wondering at what period the portraits of herself and her descendants would be displaced by some other family, and the Cloptons be exiled, even from the back passage, to make room for the Wards!

SIC TRANSIT GLORIA MUNDI.

VISIT TO COMBE ABBEY, WARWICKSHIRE.

THIS pleasant old mansion, the seat of the Earl of Craven, which lies about four miles from Coventry, besides its own particular attractions as a good specimen of an old monastic building, and containing a considerable number of valuable paintings, lying also in a pleasant park, and retaining its gardens in their primitive state—making it altogether a very agreeable spot to visit on a summer's day, with cheerful hearts and cheerful friends—has a great deal of interest attached to it, through its having been the scene of some of the earliest and latest fortunes of the Princess Elizabeth, the daughter of James I. and Queen of Bohemia. It was hence that the conspirators of the Gunpowder Plot endeavoured to seize and carry her off when a mere girl, and it was hither she returned after all the troubles of her most troublesome and disastrous reign, and enjoyed the only peaceful days of her existence. Elizabeth was a Stuart, and, like the rest of her family, was doomed to drink deep of

misfortunes; but, strictly virtuous and highly amiable, Providence seemed to concede to her what so
few of her family were permitted, or indeed deserved, a quiet termination of a stormy life.   If
ever the finger of an ill fate, laid on evil deeds,
was, however, manifest, it was not merely in her
family, but in the families of those who were concerned in the attempt to carry her off from this
place.   Such were the singular fortunes connected
with that circumstance and its great cause, the
Gunpowder Plot, that, perhaps, no other spot of
the strangely eventful soil of England can show
more remarkable ones.   It will be curious to trace
these most uncommon and melancholy facts before
we make our visit to the house.

    The Princess Elizabeth was, at the time of the
plot, living here under the care of the Earl of Harrington, the then proprietor of the abbey.   This
circumstance, and the fact also that several of the
conspirators were closely connected with that part
of the country, drew them in their defeat in that
direction, and made Warwickshire, with its neighbouring counties of Worcester and Stafford, the
grand scene of the catastrophe.

    It appears singular, at first view, that so many
of the principal conspirators were from the the midland counties; but Worcestershire, Staffordshire,

and Warwickshire, were inhabited by more stanch Catholic families than perhaps any other part of England. Warwickshire, moreover, never was conspicuous for its attachment to the Stuarts, as was eminently shown when the Parliament and Charles I. came to open rupture. Catesby, the originator of the plot, was, indeed, of Ashby St. Legers in Northamptonshire,—itself, however, not far distant from the scene of action, and he was intimately connected with the Catholics in these counties. In his case, as very remarkably in that of several others of the conspirators, and as is more often the fact in life than we are aware of till we begin to trace back effects to their causes, he was in a great degree the victim of his father's crimes and a pernicious education. He was lineally descended from that Catesby, who was the favourite and one of the base ministers of Richard III., whose fame is still preserved in the old popular rhyme:

> The Rat, the Cat, and Lovel the dog,
> Rule all England under the Hog.

He appears to have been one of the most zealous and devoted bigots that this country ever produced. He was for many years the sworn friend of Gar-

net, the principal of the Jesuits in England, and
was supposed to be concerned, more or less, in all
the plots and schemes of treason which fermented
and occasionally came to the light during the reign
of Elizabeth. On her death, the hopes of the Catholics rose high. James, the son of Mary Queen of
Scots, a queen who had suffered so much from the
heretic Elizabeth, and a queen, too, so fervently
attached to the Catholic religion, was fondly expected by the Papists, when seated on the throne
of Great Britain, and free to avow his own predi-
lections, to show that the influence of blood and of
filial resentment were not unfelt. They hoped from
him, if not the restoration of the ancient worship,
at least a most indulgent toleration of it. James
disappointed them. He showed every disposition
to put into rigorous force the laws against popish
recusants; and when, on the conclusion of a peace
with the king· of Spain, even that monarch was
found to have secured no stipulation in favour of
the English Catholics, their rage and disappoint-
ment grew desperate. Catesby hit upon the grand
idea of blowing the whole Protestant government
of England into the air. He soon found in Thomas
Percy, a branch of the illustrious house of Northumberland, a ready coadjutor, for Percy was
smarting under personal resentments towards the

king, and already brooding on a plan of assassination.

One of the earliest to join these desperate men in so desperate an enterprise, was a gentleman who, at first sight, would have seemed the most unlikely of all persons, and that was the handsome, the accomplished, the fortunate—and, as far as personal disposition, the resources of mind and of fortune, elegant pursuits, and the dearest domestic ties, could make any man so—the singularly happy Sir Everard Digby.

Sir Everard was descended of a highly distinguished line. He was distinguished at the court of Elizabeth, by the graces of his person, and his accomplishments; from James himself he had received the honour of knighthood. His father had made himself known by his philosophical writings, and he himself had received such an education, and possessed such abilities as made the path of fresh honours easy and alluring. As if fortune had intended to mark him out as one of her especial favourites, he had succeeded in gaining the hand of a woman, at once of great endowments of person, mind, and estate,—the sole heiress of the Mulsho family, of Gothurst in Buckinghamshire. To crown this extraordinary tendency towards felicity, he had already two lovely children; one

of them afterwards destined to acquire great distinction for himself, as Sir Kenelm Digby. What
then was the disastrous cause which was able to
overpower all these concurrent auspices, and lead
him into this bloody enterprise? An unlucky
education. His father died when he was but
eleven years old, and the priests of the Catholic
families with which he was most intimately connected, seized on the opportunity to mould his
naturally fine and generous mind to the views of
their party. They brought him up with the most
devoted notions of the claims of the Catholic
church, and the duties which every gentleman in
this country owed it; and he eventually became
the victim of these their inculcations.

But there was another circumstance, and one
which I have here more particularly in view,
which, to a mind accustomed to mark such things
in the current of human affairs, might seem to have
a mysterious influence.

In the old park of Coleshill, in Warwickshire,
formerly stood the ancient hall of the De Montfords.
In the reign of Henry VII., Sir Simon de Montford
was accused of sending 30l. to Perkin Warbeck,
whom he firmly believed to be the son of Edward
IV. He was tried at Guildhall in 1494, for high
treason, condemned, hanged, and quartered at

Tyburn, and all his vast estates confiscated. The
people beheld with surprise that he who had been
the accuser of De Montford at the bar—Simon
Digby, keeper of the Tower, speedily become the
possessor of his estate at Coleshill, and established himself as master in his ancient house there.
In this very house, according to tradition, a descendant of this Simon Digby, who attained it by
the destruction of its lawful lord, on a plea of high
treason, was wont to hold secret councils with
Catesby and his fellows, concocting a scheme of
treason of the most terrible description, and which
brought him to the block when all other circumstances tended to his felicity and advancing fortune.

But the most striking instance of that fatality
which seems to linger in criminal families for some
generations, yet at length breaks out, and " visits
the sins of the father on the children even unto the
third and fourth generation," was shown in yet
another family—that of Lyttleton—which furnished
two traitor-victims to this popish plot.

At Shirford, near Nuneaton, in Warwickshire,
there formerly stood an old hall, now long since
fallen to decay and pulled down, which, with a fair
estate there, belonged to a most unfortunate family
of the Smiths.

About the middle of the sixteenth century, Sir

Walter Smith was the possessor of Shirford Manor,
and his singular story is thus related by Sir William Dugdale: " Sir Walter, being grown an
aged man at the death of his first wife, and considering of a marriage for Richard, his son and
heir, then grown up to man's estate, made his mind
known to Mr. Thomas Chetwyn, of Ingestrie in
Staffordshire, a gentleman of ancient family and
fair estate, who, encouraging the proposal in behalf
of one of his daughters, Dorothy, was willing to
give five hundred pounds, as a portion with her.
But, no sooner had the old knight seen the young
lady, than he became a suitor for himself; being so
captivated with her beauty, that he tendered as
much for her, besides a good jointure, as he should
have received in case the match had gone for his
son; which liberal offer so wrought upon Mr.
Chetwyn as that he spared not for arguments to
persuade his daughter to accept of Sir Walter for
her husband ;—whereupon the marriage ensued accordingly ; but with what a tragic issue will quickly
be seen : for it was not long ere that, her affections
wandering after younger men, she gave entertainment to one Mr. William Robinson, then of Drayton
Basset, a young gentleman of about twenty-two
years of age, son of Sir George Robinson, a rich
mercer of London ; and grew so impatient of all

impediments which might hinder her full enjoyment
of him, that she rested not till she had contrived a
way to be rid of her husband. For which purpose,
corrupting her waiting-gentlewoman and a groom
of the stable, she resolved, by their help and the
assistance of Robinson, to strangle him in bed, ap-
pointing a time and manner how it should be effected. And though Robinson failed in coming on
the designed night, perhaps through a right apprehension of so direful a fact, she no whit staggered
in her resolutions; for, watching her husband till he
had fallen asleep, she let in the assassins before
specified ; and casting a long towel about his neck,
caused the groom to lie upon him to keep him from
struggling, whilst herself and her maid, straining
the towel, stopped his breath.

"It seems the good old man little thought that
his lady had acted therein ; for when they first cast
the towel about his neck, he cried out, ' Help, Doll,
help !' After an hour, that the maid and groom
were silently got away, to palliate the business, she
made an outcry in the house, wringing her hands,
pulling her hair, and weeping extremely, with pre-
tence that she had found him in that condition.
Which subtle and feigned show of sorrow prevented all suspicions of his violent death ; and, not
long after she went to London, setting so high a

value upon her beauty, that Robinson her former
darling, perhaps for not keeping touch with her, as
before hath been said, became neglected.   But,
within two years following, it so happened that this
woeful deed of darkness was brought to light by
the groom before specified, who, being entertained
with Mr. Richard Smith, son and heir to the murdered knight; and, attending him to Coventry with
divers other servants, became so sensible of his
villany when he was in his cups, that, out of good-
nature, he took his master aside, and upon his
knees, besought forgiveness from him for acting in
the murder of his father, declaring all the circumstances thereof.   Wherefore Mr. Smith discreetly
gave him good words, but wished some others that
he trusted to have an eye to him, that he might not
escape when he had slept and better considered
what might be the issue thereof.   Notwithstanding
which direction, he fled away with his master's best
horse, and hasting into Wales, attempted to go beyond sea; but, being hindered by contrary winds,
after three essays to launch out, was so happily
pursued by Mr. Smith, who spared no cost in sending to several ports, that he was found out and
brought prisoner to Warwick, as was also the lady
and her gentlewoman, all of whom with great bold-
ness denying the fact, and the groom most impu-

dently charging Mr. Smith with endeavour of corrupting him to accuse the lady, his mother-in-law, falsely, to the end that he might get her jointure. But upon his arraignment, so smitten was he at the apprehension of the guilt, that he publicly acknowledged it, and stoutly justified what he had so said to be true, to the face of the lady and her maid: who, at first, with much seeming confidence pleaded their innocence, till, at length, seeing the particular circumstances thus discovered, they both confessed the fact. For which, having judgment to dye, the lady was burnt at a stake, near the Hermitage on Wolvey-heath, towards the side of Shirford lordship, where the country people to this day show the place; and the groom, with the maid, suffered death at Warwick."

But misfortune had not yet done with this family. This Richard Smith, having avenged the death of his father, it came to his turn, in the course of years, to become the prey of Sir John Lyttleton, who, to use the words of Sir William Dugdale, " juggled him out of a fair inheritance," of which this lordship of Shirford formed a part. We cannot do better than let Sir William tell this most singular story, as he has done the last.

" Having but one daughter, called Margaret, by

his first wife, and doubting of male issue, he treated
with Sir John Lyttleton, of Frankley in Worcestershire, for a marriage betwixt his said daughter and
William Lyttleton, third son of the said Sir John;
in consideration of which he agreed to settle all his
lands in remainder, after his own decease, without
other issue, upon the said William and Margaret,
and their heirs.   And having writings drawn accordingly, trusted the said Sir John Lyttleton to get
them engrossed.   Which being effected, and a day
appointed for sealing, Mr. Smith came to Frankley,
where he found a very noble entertainment, and
some of Sir John's friends to bear him company, in
whose presence the writings were brought forth,
and begun to be read : but before they came to the
uses, stept in Sir John Lyttleton's keeper in a sweat,
and told them that there were a brace of bucks at
lair in the park, which carried a glass in their tails
for Mr. Smith's dogs to look in—for he loved
coursing well, and had his grayhounds there—but
if they made not haste, those market-people which
passed through the park would undoubtedly rouse
them.   Wherefore Sir John Lyttleton earnestly
moved Mr. Smith to seal the writings without further reading, protesting that they were according
to the draughts he had seen, and without any altera-

tion. Which bold asseverations, putting him out of all suspicion of sinister dealing, caused him forthwith to seal them, and to go into the park.

" Hereupon the two children, for they were each of them not above nine years old, were married together, and lived in the house with Sir John. But it so happened that, about six years after, the young man died by a fall from his horse, insomuch as Mr. Smith, considering that his daughter had no issue, resolved to take her away, and signified as much to Sir John; who, designing to marry her again to George, his second son, refused to deliver her; till which time Mr. Smith never suspected any thing in the deed, formerly so sealed, as hath been said. But then, upon difference between him and Sir John, it appeared that for want of issue by the before specified William and Margaret, the lands were to devolve unto the right heirs of the said William, which was Gilbert Lyttleton, the eldest brother, contrary to the plain agreement at first made. To make short, therefore, William, the third son, married her—George, the second son, enjoyed her—and Gilbert, the eldest, had the estate, as heir to his brother."

From Gilbert, the eldest son of this bold bad man, the estate descended to his son John, from whom Mr. Smith in vain endeavoured to recover it

by several suits at law. Misfortune descended
with it. John Lyttleton, the son of Gilbert, being
attainted for high treason for uniting with the Earl
of Essex in the 42d of Elizabeth, and this very
estate was forfeited to the crown. It was afterwards granted by James I. to the widow of John
Lyttleton, on her petition; and she, being justly ap-
prehensive of fresh law-suits from Smith, sold it to
Serjeant Hale, a lawyer of great eminence. Hale
disposed of it among his five sons,—but the curse
of unjust possession seemed divided amongst them
with it; it became a source of most bitter and in-
extinguishable contentions amongst them.

Nor did the ill luck confine itself to one line of
the juggling Sir John Lyttleton's descendants; another of his grandsons—Stephen, the son of his
second son George and of this Margaret Smith,
became one of the chief conspirators in the Gunpowder Plot, and lost his life and estates in consequence. His cousin Humphry, the younger brother
of that John who had suffered attainder for his par-
ticipation in Essex's affair, a conspirator, too, narrowly escaping with his own life in endeavouring
to save Stephen.

If ever a fatality attended ill-gotten property,
surely it did that of this daring Sir John Lyttleton.
The very means which the Lyttletons used seemed

to become the means for their destruction, and their dishonour was brought, as it were by the design and agency of some supernatural power, to their own country, and exhibited before the eyes of their neighbours.   Nay, as treason and gunpowder were employed by them, treason and gunpowder brought them to their fate.

The course of these strange circumstances now lead us to Combe Abbey.   The plot being all ready, and the whole of the royal family being expected to be blown up—except the Duke of York, whom Percy was to seize, and the Princess Elizabeth, who was here—Sir Everard Digby undertook to be at Dunchurch with a body of horse raised amongst his friends thereabout, and seize upon the princess.   As she was a child, and therefore not too old to be educated in the Catholic faith, her they proposed to proclaim queen.   When the day came, and, instead of the blowing up of the Parliament, the discovery of the plot was made, and Guy Fawkes seized; Catesby, Percy, the Lyttletons, and others of the conspirators, as if struck with infatuation, instead of making their escape abroad, all hastened down to Dunchurch to Sir Everard Digby, in the wild hope of seizing the princess, and raising a civil war in her name.   The princess, by the activity of Lord Harrington, was

conveyed into Coventry. The celebrated Sir Fulke
Greville, who was deputy-lieutenant of the county,
appeared in force against them. He seized the
horses, arms, and persons of the suspected; the
sheriff raised the country; and the unhappy conspirators soon found the population from whom
they had vainly hoped for support, up, and in full
chase of them. The pursuit was hot: gentle and
simple, cavalry and peasantry, came fiercely upon
them from all quarters, and they flew in wild confusion across the county into Worcestershire; some
taking shelter in Hendlip-hall, the seat of Thomas
Habington, Esq., a zealous Catholic and a secret
favourer of their views, but the greater number
fleeing to Holbeach-house, the fortified mansion of
Stephen Lyttleton.

The account of the discovery of those who concealed themselves at Hendlip, as given in the
" Beauties of England," vol. xv., is very curious.
The Habingtons were a family of great distinction
and talent. The then owner, Thomas, was a man
of letters. He wrote a history of Edward VI.,
which was completed by his son William Habington, the author of Castara, in which he celebrated
under that name, his wife Lucia, the daughter of
William Lord Powis; a poem which went through
several editions at the time, and which has been

reprinted in the present century by Mr. Elton. William was author also of " The Queen of Arragon," a play acted at court before Charles I., and again at the Restoration ; on this latter occasion with a prologue and epilogue, by the author of Hudibras.

But the Habingtons were as zealously attached to the Catholic cause as to letters. Thomas, the father of the poet, and at this time possessor of Hendlip, had been deep in the Babington conspiracy for the release of the Queen of Scots, and had suffered six years imprisonment in the Tower. His brother Edward also engaged in the same conspiracy, and suffered death for it. Thomas was married to Mary, the sister of Lord Monteagle, and it is supposed to be this lady whose letter of warning to her brother led to the discovery of the plot. John Habington, the father of Thomas, and grandfather of the poet, had, even while cofferer to Queen Elizabeth, been also a secret partisan of the Queen of Scots, and supporter of the Catholic interest, and had built the hall at Hendlip in such a style as might render it, on occasion, a place of most subtle concealment. " There is," says the Beauties of England, " scarcely an apartment that has not secret ways of going in or going out; some have back stairs concealed in the walls; others

have places of concealment in the chimneys. Some
have trap-doors; and all present a picture of gloom,
insecurity, and suspicion." Something of the same
kind we shall observe in the old house of Compton
Winyates.

When the sheriff came with a party to Hendlip
to search for the fugitives, Habington stoutly denied that any of them were there; but the sheriff
was too certain to the contrary to be easily put off.
A most minute and persevering search was made,
when in the gallery over the gate there were found
two cunning and artificial conveyances in the main
brick wall, so ingeniously framed, and with such
art, as cost much labour ere they could be found.
Three other secret places, contrived with no less
skill and industry, were found in and about the
chimneys, in one whereof two of the traitors were
close concealed. These chimney conveyances
being so strangely formed, having the entrances
into them so curiously covered with brick, mor-
tared and made fast to planks of wood, and
coloured black like the other part of the chimney,
that very diligent inquisition might well have
passed by without throwing the least suspicion on
such unsuspicious places. And whereas divers
funnels are usually made to chimneys according
as they are combined together, and serve for the

necessary use in several rooms, where were some
that exceeded common expectation, seeming out-
wardly fit for carrying forth smoke; but being further examined and seen into, the service was to no
such purpose, but only to lend light and air downwards into the concealment where such as should
be enclosed in them any time should be hidden.
Eleven such corners and conveyances were found
in the said house, all of them having books, mass-
ing stuff, and trumpery in them, only two ex-
cepted, which appeared to have been found in
some former search, and therefore had now the
less credit given to them.

" Three days had been fully spent, and no more
found there all this while; but upon the fourth day
in the morning, from behind the wainscot in the
galleries came forth two men of their own volun-
tary accord, as being no longer able to conceal
themselves; for they confessed that they had but
one apple between them, which was all the suste-
nance they had received during the time they were
there hidden. One of them was named Owen, who
afterwards murdered himself in the Tower, and
the other Chambers. On the eighth day, the be-
fore-mentioned place in the chimney was found.
Forth of this secret and most cunning conveyance
came Henry Garnet, the Jesuit sought for, and

another with him named Hall ;* marmalade and
other sweetmeats were found there lying by them,
but their better maintenance was by a quill or reed,
through a little. hole in the chimney that backed
another chimney into a gentlewoman's chamber,
and by that passage caudles, broths, and warm
drinks had been conveyed to them."

But the most singular fortune befel the Lyttletons.
They, with Sir Everard Digby and a considerable
number of the other conspirators, made good their
flight to Holbeach House, the seat of Stephen Lyttleton, where they determined to make a desperate
resistance ; but by a curious coincidence, the very
death which they had intended for the king and
parliament, had nearly been their own,—their gunpowder, by some accident, exploded, blew up the
roof, wounded some of them, and rendered the
house untenable.   There was nothing left but to
make a bold sally, in which Stephen Lyttleton
and Winter made their escape, but Percy, Catesby,
and some others were killed, and Sir Everard
Digby and the rest made prisoners.

Stephen Lyttleton and Winter, though they had
escaped immediate death or captivity, were in a
condition little better.   They were in a country

* This Jesuit, called also Alcuine, or Oldcorn, was domes-
ticated in the family.

swarming with active enemies in quest of them, and were obliged to skulk in woods, and hide them-' selves from view in a miserable condition of hourly fear and starvation. At length Humphry, the cousin of Stephen Lyttleton, conducted them to Hagley, then the house of the widow of his late unfortunate brother John, by which he rashly endangered the very property which had been recently restored to her by the king. Luckily, however, she was absent, and could not be held accountable for their entering there; and there, moreover, they soon found that treason in a servant which they had entertained against the whole body of the government; and were delivered up to their fate.

So perished this singular body of conspirators, many of them closing with a fearful catastrophe, very remarkable histories, and what is not less remarkable, the lines of Digby and Lyttleton, as if sufficient expiation had now been made for their ancestral crimes, again extended in dignity and prosperous state.

The Princess Elizabeth, thus rescued from the meditated grasp of the conspirators here in her youth, returned once more to Combe Abbey in her latter days. Like that of all the Stuarts, her fate had a melancholy hue. The story of her unfortu-

nate husband, Frederick, the Elector Palatine, of
his being raised to the crown of Bohemia; of his
struggles to maintain his elevation, in which he
was left without the smallest aid by his cold-
blooded and pedantic father-in-law, James I.} of
his dethronement and melancholy end, is well-
known to most readers. If Elizabeth knew any
enjoyment of life, it must have been in those later
days when she resided in England. Many English
gentlemen had chivalrously fought to maintain the
cause of her and her husband in this kingdom, and
amongst them she found a most devoted friend in
the then Lord Craven. She is supposed, during
her residence in this country, to have been pri-
vately married to him, and she left him her collection of paintings, most of which are here. In the
great gallery of the house, the portraits of her husband and herself are surrounded by those of almost
every individual of her own family, the Stuarts,
and of most of those gallant officers, English and
German, who distinguished themselves in their
endeavours to maintain the Elector on the throne
of Bohemia.

The great interest of this house consists, indeed,
in its connexion with the history of this amiable but
unfortunate princess. The beautiful but dissipated
Margravine of Anspach, whose portrait will be

found on the staircase, may excite a momentary
attention, but the mind will here speedily revert to
Elizabeth, and every room of the house will present
you with the characters and memorials of her
story. In the Breakfast Room are white marble
busts of Elizabeth and her daughter the Princess
Sophia. In the Great Gallery are portraits of a
daughter of Charles I.; Dukes of Richmond and
Brunswick; Charles I.; Charles II. at fourteen;
Earl of Craven; Prince Edward, Count Palatine;
the Queen of Bohemia herself, a half-length by
Honthorst, a very different face to that of the full-
length at Hampton Court attributed to the same
artist. She has here all the Stuart countenance;
an amiable but melancholy look, her crown on her
head, and is robed in ermine. There is also a head
of the king; of Gustavus Adolphus, the king's firm
friend; Honthorst, the painter to the court of
Bohemia, by himself; a great number of the officers who fought in the king's wars; the queen's
daughter as an abbess; Charles II. and James II.,
and their queens; Princes Rupert and Maurice,
and Dukes of Richmond and Brunswick again;
Duke of Richmond again, full-length; Prince
Henry. In the Bohemia Room, you have the
queen again, full-length, with six daughters and
four sons. In the Vandyke Room, are the Coun-

tess of Bedford, the daughter of Lord Harrington,
who was educated with the Princess Elizabeth;
two daughters of Elizabeth. On the Staircase are
Rupert and Maurice again; a fine portrait of Lord
Craven, and another in armour; Duchess of Or-
leans, daughter of Charles I., by Vandyke. In the
Library, Charles II. in buff and cuirass; the
Duchess of Cleveland, said to be by three masters,
Lely, Dobson, and Kneller. In the Drawing Room,
full-lengths of the King and Queen of Bohemia, by
Honthorst. The king is represented in armour,
with a surcoat of velvet lined with ermine. The
sceptre is in his hand, and the crown, which was a
most uneasy one to him, on his head. It is a fine
portrait, expressing great mildness of character.
Elizabeth is in black, richly adorned with pearls.
We have here again Charles I., by Mytens;
and full-lengths of Maurice and Rupert, in their
youth, in buff. In the Beauty Parlour, so called
from the portraits of the beauties of Charles II.'s
court formerly hanging there, are now Charles I.
and his queen, three-quarter-lengths, by Vandyke,
painted at the request of Elizabeth. They are
crowned, and Henrietta is presenting Charles with
a laurel-wreath. The king was evidently drawn
in an hour of domestic comfort; and his countenance is more cheerful and happy than you see it

anywhere else. In the Hunting Parlour, are the beauties of Charles II.'s court. They are said, many of them, to be by Lely, but they are merely small heads, and not very striking.

Perhaps so many portraits of the Stuart family are not to be met with in any one place besides, as these which were chiefly collected by the affection of Elizabeth. There is none, indeed, like the grand equestrian Vandykes of Charles I. at Warwick Castle, Windsor, and Hampton Court; but there are many of a high character, and some nowhere else to be found. These render a visit to Combe well worth making; but besides these the Abbey contains many admirable subjects by first-rate masters. Vandyke, Reubens, Carravagio, Lely, Kneller, Brughel, Teniers, Mereveldt, Paul Veronese, Rembrandt, Holbein, and Albert Durer. Amongst them I may particularly mention fine and characteristic portraits of Sir Kenelm Digby, Sir Thomas More, General Monk, Lord Strafford, Vandyke by himself, Honthorst by himself; heads of the Saxony Reformers, by a Saxon artist; Lot and his daughter, by Michael Angelo. There is also a very curious old picture of a lady with a golden drinking horn in her hand, and a Latin legend of Count Otto, who hunting in the forest, and seeing this lady, asked to drink out of her horn, for he was dreadfully athirst; but on looking into it, he was suspicious of the liquor, and pouring it behind him, part of it fell on his horse, and took off the hair like fire.

The Gallery is a fine old wainscoted room; the cloisters are now adorned with projecting antlers of stags, and black-jacks. There are old tapestry, old paintings, old cabinets, one made of ebony, tortoise-shell, and gold; and the house altogether has that air, and those vestiges of old times which must, independent of the Queen of Bohemia, give it great interest in the eyes of the lovers of old English houses, and of the traces of past generations.

Mrs. Jameson, in her interesting "Visits at Home and Abroad," thus speaks of Elizabeth and of the most striking event in her history, that of occasioning the celebrated "Thirty Years' War."

"MEDON.—Do you forget that the cause of the Thirty Years' War was a woman?

"ALDA.—A woman and religion; the two best or worst things in the world, according as they are understood and felt, used and abused. You allude to Elizabeth of Bohemia, who was to Heidelberg what Helen was to Troy.

" One of the most interesting monuments of Heidelberg, at least to an English traveller, is the elegant triumphal arch raised by the Palatine Frederic V. in honour of his bride—this very Elizabeth Stuart. I well remember with what self-complacency and enthusiasm our Chief walked about in a heavy rain, examining, dwelling upon every trace of this celebrated and unhappy woman. She had been educated at his country seat, and one of the avenues of his magnificent park yet bears her name. On her, fell a double portion of the miseries of her fated family. She had the beauty and the wit, the gay spirits, the elegant tastes, the kindly disposition of her grandmother, Mary of Scotland. Her very virtues, as a wife and a woman, not less than her pride and feminine prejudices, ruined herself, her husband, and her people. When Frederic hesitated to accept the crown of Bohemia, his high-spirited wife exclaimed, ' Let me rather eat dry bread at a king's table than feast at the board of an elector;' and it seemed as if some avenging demon hovered in the air, to take her literally at her word, for she and her family lived to eat dry bread; ay, and to beg it before they ate

18*

it; but she *would* be a queen. Blest as she was in
love, in all good gifts of nature and fortune, in all
means of happiness, a kingly crown was wanting
to complete her felicity; and it was cemented to
her brow with the blood of two millions of men.
And who was to blame? Was not her mode of
thinking the fashion of her time, the effect of her
education? Who had

> Put in her tender heart the aspiring flame
> Of golden sovereignty !"

VISIT TO LINDISFARNE, FLODDEN FIELD, AND OTHER SCENERY OF MARMION.

THE poetry of Scott has been eclipsed by his prose. He had the singular fortune to see his poetic fame diminished by a cause which carried with it its own consolation,—the vast success of those prose romances which came after his metrical ones,—prose in outward form, but abounding in all the elements of poetry, in such force and extent as gave him no mean claim to the title of the second Shakspeare. 'Twas a proud circumstance, and one which can happen rarely in the history of literature, that the gloom cast upon his poetry, after it had placed him by acclamation in the chair of cotemporary supremacy, was the mighty shadow of his own growing form, as he ascended higher and still higher up the mountain of Fame, and towards the sun of universal favour. There was indeed another cause which operated collaterally to put down his romantic lays below their just position, and that was the novelty, and consequent

great popularity of Byron's Eastern Tales. This
cause could, however, have produced merely a
temporary effect; for the exaggerated and un-
healthy spirit of the Giaour and Mazeppa school
could not long maintain its hold upon the public
mind. The very effect of Byron's other productions tended to destroy their influence; for it was
impossible for the same mind to feel the philosophic
depth and spiritual beauty of Childe Harold, or of
Cain, or to enjoy the wit, the humour, the sarcasm,
the graphic painting of human life, the alternating
mockery and poetic feeling which characterize the
equally wonderful and reprehensible Don Juan, and
still to admire the stilted and hectoring style of
those Turkish tales. Byron was himself the first
to laugh at the public which had swallowed his
mock-heroic for the true sublime. Between the
other poetry of Byron and that of Scott there could
be no direct comparison, and therefore no unjust
disparagement; for, though no one would contest
the question of Byron's superiority, as a poet, to
Scott, no intellect which could feel the greatness of
the one could be insensible to the real merit of the
other in any of his productions. It could only be
the fascination of the prose romances of Scott
which could draw away the public from his poetical
ones, and make it for a time unjust in its estimate

of them; for, after all, in their particular class and department, they are amongst the most delightful poems in the language. They are not poetry of the grade of Shakspeare's Hamlet or Lear, of Milton's Paradise lost, or some of the writings of Wordsworth or Coleridge; they do not fix us in deep astonishment as does the stern majesty of some of these, nor lead us down into the deepest regions of the human heart as do the others; yet they are, in their way and of their kind, as real poetry. They are transcripts of nature in her most beautiful scenery, of human life in its most picturesque and romantic shape. Who would wish for ever to be borne along by the city crowd, to live amid the fiercest political agitations, within the sound of the most trenchant or patriotic eloquence, whether of senate or of bar, and would not delight to steal away to the domestic fireside—to home, peace and affection, to the voices of children, wives, sisters, and friends? There are none but feel the delicious charm of such retreat from the excitement and exasperation of those public stimulants, and none therefore but who must love the poetry of Scott. The epistles prefatory to each canto of Marmion are some of the most interesting peeps into a heart, strong in its tastes and warm in its affections, with which the world was ever favoured.

It is an old truth, that we may have too much of a good thing; and to climb Alps, however magnificent,—to wander amid the stunning roar of an ocean, however sublime,—to run bareheaded through tempests and darkness, however exciting, can be only the wild delights of a moment,—acts of youth, of passion, or romance; but, to stroll out for a summer evening, amongst beautiful hills, by streams rapid and clear; through forests hoary with years, yet green and musical with spring; these are refreshments which every day and every stage of life have enough in them of weariness and annoyance to render most welcome, and all who love them must love the poetry of Scott. He himself knew, as well as any man, the genuine character and claims of his poetry. He took down from the crumbling wall of the feudal castle, the disused harp of the old metrical romancer, and strung it again to feudal strains in the improved harmony of modern language, and with the wider views of modern society. If the field was old, the mode of its occupation was new: he engrafted on the old Anglo-Norman stock, a germ of poetry novel and peculiar. Chivalrous life, as seen not from its own living centre, but from the modern distance, was beheld again with a quick delight which proved the original power and fresh feeling of its restorer.

And had it no high and heroic excitement? The life and character of the Gael and the Borderer, till then nearly overlooked; the adventures of Bruce, Wallace, and the fourth and fifth James; the contentions of England and Scotland; the beauty of the highland hills and lochs, and the stern picturesqueness of many a mouldering castle, both in highland and lowland,—all had a newness, a piquancy, and a spirit in them, that was felt throughout the kingdom. It is true that, as to heroic story and human character in all its varieties, the abandonment of rhythmical restraint subsequently enabled him to sketch more broadly, and fill up more freely and fully; but after all, when that reaction takes place, which assuredly will, it will be found that there is no poetry so thoroughly imbued with that species of beauty which every summer leads so many thousands to the Scottish highlands, as that of the man whose very name seems to designate him, *par excellence*, THE SCOTT. His poetry actually smells of the heather.* I never read it, or think of it, but I hear the very rustle of the crimson heath-bells in the gale. I see the beautiful birches dipping their pensile boughs in summer waters as beautiful. Around me are moss and ferns, where the roebuck couches in secret; before me, scattered over the brown waste, little brown huts, part and parcel of the scene, sending abroad the odour of their peat-fires; and my imagination is haunted by shapes of highland warriors, watching to accomplish some stern design, or fairies that still take a peep at this steam-engine world from the hidden entrance to their pleasant subterrane.

So much for a passing tribute to the. poetry of Scott, which, like that of Southey, has for a time been underrated, because we had got the metaphysical fit upon us, and could not condescend to be pleased except with what required reading twice over. Happy is the man whose taste is not so exclusive, but who has eyes for beauty wherever it is to be found, in all fields and schools, whether pleasant or profound !

The poem of Marmion has always been reckoned the highest in merit amongst those of Scott, as more active, bustling and spirited than the rest. If it were only for those introductory epistles, it ought to be dear to every feeling heart. Where is the spirit of a genuine friendship so sensibly-felt; where are those descriptions of country life so living, especially in those gloomy months which stir the imagination of the poetical?

Heap on more wood, the wind is chill ;
But let it whistle as it will,
We'll keep our merry Christmas still.

Christmas, indeed, never was so richly painted as in this letter to Richard Heber; and what sportsman, or country gentleman, does not feel the truth of the following lines?—

> When sylvan occupation's done,
> And on the chimney rests the gun;
> And, hung in idle trophy near,
> The game-pouch, fishing-rod, and spear;
> When wiry terrier, rough and grim,
> And greyhound with his length of limb,
> And pointer, now employed no more,
> Cumber our parlour's narrow floor;
> When in his stall the impatient steed,
> Is long condemned to rest and feed;
> When from our snow-encircled home,
> Scarce cares the hardiest step to roam,
> Since path is none, save that to bring
> The needful water from the spring;
> When wrinkled news-page, thrice conned o'er,
> Beguiles the dreary hour no more;
> And darkling politician crossed,
> Inveighs against the lingering post,
> And answering housewife sore complains
> Of carriers' snow-impeded wains.
>
> *Introduction to Canto V.*

Hogg himself has not laid before us the wintry toils and perils of the mountain shepherd more

vividly than does his letter preceding canto fourth.
He induces us to ask with him,

> Who envies now the shepherd's lot,
> His healthy fare, his rural cot,
> His summer couch by greenwood tree,
> His rustic kirn's loud revelry,
> His native wood-notes tuned on high
> To Marion of the blithesome eye ;
> His crook, his scrip, his oaten reed,
> And all Arcadia's golden creed !

The very foundation of the poet's own character
and tastes are all sketched out in these letters with
a most delightful feeling. In the poem itself, it is
not to be denied that there are many passages of
merely easy tinkling rhyme, but there are also
many others of the richest harmony and of the
true trumpet tone. But we must pass from the poem
to the scenery of its action. Not, however, let us
premise here, to go over all that ground, for it
would lead us to Edinburgh, to Boroughmoor, to
Tantallon, and a whole train of places where our
excellent friend Robert Chambers can lead the
reader a thousand times better ; being one of those
rare persons whose love of antiquities has grown,
like that of Scott himself, out of the poetical feeling,

and who has, in indulgence of it, traced some thousands of miles of auld Scotland, and made many
a nook of Edinburgh as familiar to him as the face
of his Journal is to his host of readers. We must
confine ourselves to the two most important points
of interest, Holy Isle and Flodden Field.

LINDISFARNE IN HOLY ISLAND.

NEXT to the great natural interest which bears
upon the Battle of Flodden, is that produced by the
fate of Constance de Beverley in the dungeon of
Lindisfarne Abbey. In this episode Scott has por-
trayed one of those horrid practices of the Catholic
church in its days of unlimited power, which
forcibly act upon the imagination, because they are
surrounded with mystery and darkness, and involve
their destinies in a machinery so vast and overwhelming as to present no result to the sufferers but
despair and death. This scene in the dungeon of
Lindisfarne is one of the most intensely interesting
and powerfully painted in English poetry. The
victims, a young, beautiful, and faithful, but ill re-
quited woman, roused by the passions of love, and

jealousy, and resentment, to deeds against her rival
of a deadly character, and the sordid wretch by
whom she strove to accomplish her vengeance.
The high spirit of the woman, which rises and
towers over the heads of her judges in majesty
of injured feeling, and the base fear of the man,

> Who shamed not loud to moan and howl;
> His body on the floor to dash,
> And crouch like hound beneath the lash,

contrast finely, as does the impassioned eloquence
of the unhappy lady, with the awe-stricken aspects
of her judges, who pronounce the fatal words,

> Sister, let thy sorrows cease,
> Sinful brother part in peace;

and hurry up to the light of day. The place a
dungeon, whose access was a secret, except to
the abbot and a few of his familiars, a hundred
steps below the surface, where the thunder of the
ocean above it was heard as a dull sound; the
figures of the judges in their monastic robes and
seated on their stone seats; the dim cresset showing
the sepulchral vault, the two executioners and the
two niches ready to receive their living victims,

and the stones and mortar ready to build them
up—unite to raise the tone of mind to that pitch in
which even the exaggeration of the midnight pass-
ing-bell, which is made to be heard fifteen miles
off, becomes grand and imposing.

> Slow o'er the midnight wave it swung;
> Northumbrian rocks in answer rung;
> To Warkworth cell the echoes rolled,
> His beads the wakeful hermit told;
> The Bamborough peasant raised his head,
> But slept ere half a prayer he said;
> So far was heard the mighty knell,
> The stag sprung up on Cheviot Fell,
> Spread his broad nostril to the wind,
> Listed before, aside, behind,
> Then crouched him down beside the hind,
> And quaked amid the mountain fern,
> To hear that sound so dull and stern.

But Scott was aware of the excellent effect of
connecting as much of the circumjacent country
as possible with the scene of his subject. The
youthful reader of Marmion will recollect the pleasure with which he perused the description of the
voyage of the abbess of Whitby and her nuns to
Holy Isle; and no one can have passed over the
high ground of the Great North road, between Aln-
wick and Belford, without being struck with admi-

ration at the vast extent of sea and shore thence beheld, embracing nearly the very places which he has included in the following lines.

And now the vessel skirts the strand
Of mountainous Northumberland;
Towers, towns, and halls successive rise,
And catch the nuns' delighted eyes.
Monkwearmouth soon behind them lay,
And Tynemouth's priory and bay:
They marked amid her trees, the hall
Of lofty Seaton Delaval;
They saw the Blythe and Wansbeck floods
Rush to the sea through sounding woods;
They passed the tower of Widdrington,
Mother of many a valiant son;
At Coquet Isle their beads they tell
To the good saint who owned the cell.
Then did the Alne attention claim,
And Warkworth proud of Percy's name;
And next they crossed themselves to hear
The whitening breakers sound so near,
Where boiling through the rocks, they roar
On Dunstanborough's caverned shore.
Thy tower, proud Bamborough, marked they there;
King Ida's castle huge and square
From its tall rock look grimly down,
And on the swelling ocean frown.
Then from the coast they bore away,
And reached the Holy Island's bay.

We left the coach and dined at Belford, and set off for Holy Island. From the hill above the town we saw it lying off the coast below, at apparently no great distance. The distance is, nevertheless, four good miles, yet a pleasant walk through fields and past farm-houses, with the wide wild sea-view before us; to our right Bamborough Castle, on its lofty rock, and in the offing the Fern and Staple Islands. When we reached the strand, the scene was wild and solemn. Scott conducts his fair bevy' of voyagers thither at high water.

> The tide did now his flood-mark gain,
> And girdled in the saint's domain;
> For with the flow and ebb the style
> Varies from continent to isle;
> Dry-shod o'er sands twice every day
> The pilgrims to the shrine find way:
> Twice every day the waves efface
> Of staves and sandaled feet the trace.

But we arrived at low-water, and the sands between the mainland and Isle, called Fenham Flats, were partly bare and partly intersected with creeks and pools of salt water. If the pilgrims could cross twice a-day dryshod, it was more than we could do. We were told, indeed, that it might be done, but only by those who knew both the track and

the proper hour; those who are ignorant of these,
run a good chance of being set fast in quicksands,
or overtaken by the tide, for it is more than a mile
across. We imagine, too, that the holy pilgrims
were not dainty about wetting their sandals. We
found it necessary to pursue the curvature of the
shore, which forms a vast circuit at the lower end
of the inlet. From this point of view the projecting
land and the island appear a continuous range running for some miles parallel to the shore, a brown
and jagged range of rocks and sand-banks, worn
and torn by the ocean into an aspect sufficiently
savage. On our right hand run these sand-banks,
high, and thrown up in irregular heaps, and overgrown with sea-grass, behind them the ocean
booming with an awful grandeur. The strand was
rent and undermined by the violence of the tides.
In some places patches of smooth turf overhung
the beach, crimson with flowering thrift; in others
huge masses of the sward were lying half-buried
in the sands. The sand-hills were at intervals
scooped into caves by the assaulting ocean; an old
boat lay half buried in the sandy drift; and long
heaps of sea-weeds, shells, and pebbles, at high-
water mark, added to the picturesque effect of the
scene. Near these sand-hills we found the strand
dry, and as we advanced,—

Higher and higher rose to view,
The castle with its battled walls,
The ancient monastery's halls,
A solemn, huge, and dark-red pile,
Placed on the margin of the isle :

and besides these appeared a solitary hut on the
sandy promontory, and two tall white obelisks,—
land-marks which kept continually varying their
apparent relative position in that singular manner
that most of my readers must have noticed. We
reached the hut, and wished for the pencil of Collins to preserve the aspect of it and its locality. It
was a fisherman's abode, erected in this wilderness
of sand-hills, with all those adjuncts of boats, nets,
pitch-casks, and remnants of fish, that are scattered about such places. There were rabbits in
abundance running in and out of their sandy bur-
rows ; and cows, which if they did not live on this
coarse and rigid sea-grass, it was a wonder on
what they did live. As we stood looking on this
isolated tenement, out came a whole troop of gro-
tesquely clad children, with the half-shy and half-
curious air that solitary children have. But this
spot was not so solitary as it seemed, for here the
promontory terminated, and across a passage of
not more than a quarter of a mile wide lay Holy
Island. On the summit of a range of dark rocks

opposite, appeared the ruins of Lindisfarne Abbey,
and to our right the castle, perched on, or rather
built into, the summit of a singular and most inac-
cessible pile of rock.   In this are stationed a few
individuals of the preventive service, and a king's
cutter is generally cruising not far off.   Some
fishermen on the island observed us, and put across
for us.   Truly a wild place, and an amphibious
population! Evening was coming fast upon us,
and no doubt greatly heightened the effect.   We
landed under a dark range of cliffs, on a shore
scattered with huge blocks fallen from above.
There were numbers of sailor-looking figures about;
boats drawn on shore, drying-houses, fish bones
scattered around, and all the signs of a fishing-
place.   We climbed the cliff, and at once appeared
the ruins of the abbey, and a village just by them.
Troops of children were at play, and their familiar
cries sounded strangely in this desolate-looking
place.   The population of the island is about five
hundred souls.   It has its school, its shops, and its
resident clergyman.   What a place for the con-
stant abode of a man of cultivated tastes! and yet
how many much more isolated stations do Christian ministers occupy, and in these kingdoms too
—in the Orkneys and Shetlands for instance.   And
how much more unselfish, how much more devoted

to the truest objects of mortal ambition and duty are they than we, if men, however lowly, however ignorant, and cut off from the ordinary haunts of society, the occupiers of the outposts of the habitable world, be still the children of one common parent, and worth seeking and gathering into the great human family.

We found the ruins of the abbey far surpassing our expectation, both in extent and beauty. They are of a massy construction, but of genuine Saxon, and in a state of preservation, their age and exposure considered, truly remarkable. The description in the poem is one of the many instances of the extreme accuracy of Sir Walter's details.

> In Saxon strength the abbey frowned,
> With massive arches broad and round,
> That rose alternate, row and row,
> *On ponderous columns, short and low,*
> Built ere the art was known,
> By pointed aisle and shafted stalk,
> The arcades of an alleyed walk
> To emulate in stone.
> On the deep walls, the heathen Dane
> Had poured his impious rage in vain;
> And needful was such strength to these,
> Exposed to the tempestuous seas,
> Scourged by the winds' eternal sway,
> Open to rovers fierce as they,

Which could twelve hundred years withstand
Winds, waves, and northern pirates' band.
Not but that portions of the pile,
Rebuilded in a later style,
Showed where the spoiler's hand had been ;
Not but the wasting sea-breeze keen,
Had worn the pillar's carving quaint,
And mouldered in his niche the saint,
And rounded, with consuming power,
The pointed angles of each tower;
Yet still entire the abbey stood,
Like veteran worn but unsubdued.

The line put in italics expresses the very peculiar character of the massy columns here. There
is a singular arch of grand dimensions, stretching
in a diagonal direction from one part of the fabric
to another, and richly adorned with the Saxon
zigzag. It appears to have been a sort of bridge-
way to some upper part of the building, reached
by a spiral staircase. The walls about the arch
itself have disappeared, and it stands in its naked
grandeur, " like a rainbow in the sky,"—on seeing
it, we exclaimed, " How like a rainbow !" " Yes,"
said the guide, "it is called the rainbow-arch. The
boys delight, above every thing, to get up and walk
across it, high and unprotected as it is. For this
reason the staircase leading to it has been built up

but still the lads will climb aloft. They stick their fingers and toes into the crevices of the masonry, and up they go."

Within the ruins of the abbey stands a rustic chapel, built from the fallen stones; and within its green inclosure rest the dead of the island. There was one circumstance which struck me in reading the inscriptions, both here and in the burying-ground of Tynemouth Priory—the numbers of deaths by shipwreck and other seafaring causes, which are recorded in these maritime cemeteries, and which makes them so different to any others. There is something both strangely fascinating to the imagination and touching to the heart in these records: so many memorials raised by the weeping spirits of the living, to husbands, brothers, sons, and lovers, whose bodies lie in the depths of the sea, and in every region of it. One is made to feel with a perception nowhere else so living, over what wastes of waters, into what far-off seas, our countrymen go. There is no part of earth or ocean whither they do not find some cause to lead them; there is no shore, desert or inhabited, where their bones do not lie: and if one could but summon around us at some one time those whose names are here, but whose bodies are absent, there would be such a combination of adventures, of sufferings and experiences, as never yet was penned in any volume.   Every stone around you has a fact upon its face which rouses a strong spirit of inquiry in your bosom.   One died in mid-sea as he was homeward bound; one perished in saving the life of another, who had fallen overboard.   One fell in a great sea-fight, whose very name is a portion of England's glory; others in desperate attempts to seize on important stations in America, North or South, the Indies, East or West.   Others were the victims of some plague-shore, that swallowed up its thousands. These died in some tropical clime; those were wrecked in sight of home, on England's own rocks.   There is no fiction, however romantic, but here finds a more striking fact; and the names of every nation and place of mercantile resort meet your eye on every hand—Chili and Mexico, Quebec and Montreal, the Straits of Magellan and the Cape of Good Hope, Newfoundland and New Zealand, are brought together in strange juxta-position in these maritime cemeteries.   And it is not only the memory of those who died thus distant that is recorded here, but the bodies of many a foreigner, and many a mariner from remote parts of England, who have been wrecked on these coasts, here take their rest.

Another cause of admiration, not the less strong, which came over us in looking on these stately ruins, was that such a fabric should be raised in such a place. What could induce the holy fathers to pitch on such desolate and isolated places in preference to the fair vales and rich lands of England ? It was a principle of action widely differing from that of the Romish church. There must have been something in the old Saxon and Celtic saints of a very primitive character. Holy Island and Iona¹ instead of the rich vales of Durham and the Lothians. It could not be the *loaves*, however it might be the *fishes*, which inspired the choice. These primitive fathers must have had a pitch of imagination highly poetical as well as religious. They must have loved the sound of the sea and the rush of the winds; they must have found inspiration in the wild aspect of crags, of naked towers, and dashing waves. They must have had pleasure in solitude and the solitary enjoyment of knowledge, or in the shepherding of souls that others cared little for, or these stately fabrics had never risen in these desolate regions. They must have had courage too; for what a sense of exposure does these islands give us, when we recollect that such savages as Norsemen and Vikinger roamed these howling seas. One no longer won-

ders at the repeated ravages committed here by the
Danes; the only wonder is that St. Cuthbert, instead
of fleeing away in his coffin, on that miraculous pilgrimage which terminated at Durham, did not flee
away on his living legs.

As we quitted the island, the gloom of evening
was upon it; the tide was rolling over the sands
between it and the mainland with whitening bil-
lows; the sea-birds were scudding about in the
gloaming with wild cries, and the roar of the ocean
beyond the sand-banks was loud and awful. The
beacon-lights on the Fern and Staples islands shone
out; and we walked on in the gathering darkness,
strongly impressed with the wildness of the scene,
and glad that we had visited it at such a time.

FLODDEN FIELD.

A fearful field in verse to frame,
    I mean, if that to mark ye list.
O Flodden Mount! thy fearful name
    Doth sore affray my trembling fist.
                    Ballad of Flodden Field.

FROM Belford to Flodden! We have got our
seven league boots on, and it is but one stride.
Nevertheless, before we move our right leg,
sheathed in our miraculous boot, we must take a
single note of a stride as marvellous. In Marmion's time, gunpowder was doing its work. One
of those ingredients out of which God works good :
it was, at the very moment that it made carnage
more horrible, breaking down the pride of physical
heroism, and the feudal system with it. It took
out of the aristocratic warrior the vanity of personal prowess, or rather personal strength, and
placed intellect, with its slave mechanical power,
far above it; and it not only took the sting of
brute force out of the feudal chief, but it
knocked down his castle about his ears. Out of
this state of things arose a new organization of

20*

civil society; the spirit of the multitude took a new
and courageous impulse. What gunpowder was
then, steam is now; and the vast projects into
which its agency is now introduced, will work
changes beyond present calculation, but assuredly
for the spread of more equal knowledge and equal
distribution of social benefits; but in the change,
there must be sufferers, and the innkeepers of the
north road could tell you their tale on this subject.
Is there any one who used to travel this road seven
years ago, who does not perceive a mighty change
on it? Who does not miss the throng of carriages
on the road, and the bustle at the inns which then
existed? In some of these large inns, which used
to have all the signs of flourishing concerns about
them, we seemed to be the solitary guests. There
were long suites of apartments, beds with their
gilded cornices, dining-rooms with their services of
plate,—but over all, the silence of desertion; servants at long intervals, and landlords with long
faces. On venturing to ask the cause, " Oh," said
our boniface, " every body now goes from the north
to London by the steamers, it is all over with post-
ing!"

We approached the Field of Flodden with great
interest. It is a place invested alike by history and
poetry with a melancholy glory. As the field most

fatal to Scotland of all those so fatally contested by that disastrous family the Stuarts; as the field where

The flowers of the forest were a' wede away,

where indeed fell twelve Scottish earls, thirteen lords, five eldest sons of peers, fifty chiefs, knights, and men of eminence, and ten thousand common men,*—it has a gloomy fame peculiar to itself. The Englishman regards it with a certain pride, as ground where the brave Earl of Surrey maintained the honour of English valour against the bravest nation and the most chivalrous monarch with which England ever contended; and the lapse of time, and the union of these two great nations into one peerless empire, have rendered the sympathies of the Englishman with that lamenting memory which dictated " the Flowers of the Forest," no longer those of a generous foe, but of a sworn brother. The blood and the interests of the two realms have

* See a detailed catalogue of the bishops, abbots, noblemen, and principal gentlemen, in " Hall's Chronicle," also quoted in Weber's edition of the stately old ballad of Flodden Field, where every thing relating to the battle and those who fought in it is brought together from the chronicles, historians and tradition.

been long enough blended into one stream, to anni-
hilate all sentiment of triumph or resentment on one
side or the other; and the inhabitants of either side
of the border, must now tread that field with no
other feelings than those of regret over the waste
of life once made there, and of thankfulness that
the cause and the occasion are done away for ever.
No one can stand here without beholding the signal
effects of the Union. The name of the field itself
is one of gloom and desolation. Our imaginations
naturally picture it as black and melancholy; to
mine no name in history or poetry had a sound so
dreary. Our astonishment was therefore proportionate to find the " dark Flodden" of the poets, so
fair and so cultivated; a scene of plentiful corn-
fields and comfortable farms. No one can, in fact,
approach, for the first time, the " Debatable Lands,"
without surprise at their extreme cultivation. That
was our feeling all through them. We directed our
course first to Wooller, where the gallant Surrey
encamped previous to the battle;

> The total army did ensue,
> And came that night to Wooler-Haugh.
> *Old Ballad of Flodden Field.*

and on reaching the eminence on the opposite side

of the valley, south-east of the town, we stood in
delighted surprise at the extensive strath, which
stretched away to our right in the highest state of
cultivation. And so we found it all along the
borders. Where the " rank reivers and moss-
troopers" used to gallop over moss and moorland,
there now stretch the richest meadows, the fairest
fields. The track which used to lie between the
two countries,—a blasted and desolate region, ra-
vaged with fire and sword, drenched with blood,
and peopled only with horrible memories,—is now
turned into a garden. The one country has blended
so beautifully into the other, that the only line of
demarcation is one of superior culture and abundance. In this neighbourhood, up to the very
ridges of the Cheviots, extend large corn-farms,
where all the improvements and scientific triumphs
of modern agriculture are displayed. How rapid
has been the recent growth of this remarkable cultivation is evidenced by statistical facts, laid before
one of "the Agricultural Committees" in parliament. There it is shown, that between 1795 and
1811, Berwickshire, a county especially exposed to
the effects of border raids formerly, had, according
to the property-tax returns, advanced from a rental
of 112,000*l.*, to 231,973*l.*; and that the following
parishes in that, and the neighbouring county of

Roxburgh, in the very neighbourhood of Flodden,
had made this striking progress :—

	Rental in 1795.	In 1836.
Whitsome parish . . £	3,080 .	. £ 7,526
Melrose	4,000 .	. 20,000
St. Boswells' . . .	1,700 .	. 3,080
Linton	2,113 .	. 5,514
Yetholm	2,104 .	. 5,600
Edrom	6,493 .	. 15,200
Eccles	11,000 .	. 20,000
	£ 30,490	£ 76,920

An increase in forty years of 166 per cent. Everywhere too, on the poorer lands on both sides the
border, planting has kept an equal pace. We
passed extensive woods, principally of pine, planted
by the Earl of Tankerville, Mr. Collingwood, Mr.
St. Paul, the Marquis of Waterford, the Duke of
Roxburgh, and many other gentlemen and noblemen. In one thing cultivation had gone too far for
us. One would have liked to see the site of so
memorable a battle respected in the general enclosure, and left as national property—as common-
able land—where the stranger, the antiquarian and
historian, might ramble at will, without trespass or
damage ; or, if this be thought too fanciful by our
modern utilitarian, that, at least, the King's-Chair

Hill itself should not be destroyed. As you advance from Millfield, you see high before you Flodden Ridge, where James first took up his position: this is now covered with a pine-wood, and is, as it should be, a conspicuous object from the country all round ; but, on arriving at that lower eminence of Branksome, whither, Pinkerton tells us that, on the morning of the battle, James, setting fire to his tents, descended, you find, to your surprise and mortification, that this very hill is in course of demolition, its very summit being turned into a stone quarry ; as if no other stone existed in this neighbourhood, or as if that, which stands as a national monument, was only worthy of mending roads and erecting pigstyes!   Whose act and deed this is we know not, but every lover of Scottish antiquities should make his most strenuous protestation against it.

Just below this King's-Chair Hill a farm-house has been erected, since the enclosure of what are called the Branksome allotments; and here is the little well which Scott has made the site of the Cross of Sybil Grey,—

A cross of stone,
That on a hillock standing lone,
Did all the field command ;

and which he has marked as the death-spot and
grave of Marmion. It is, in fact, the well which
supplies the house, and stands in the yard, so that
a good deal of the picturesque of the poet's description has gone from that, too.

> Time's wasting hand has done away
> The simple cross of Sybil Grey,
>   And broke her fount of stone ;
> And yet from out the little hill
> Oozes the slender springlet still.
>   Oft halts the stranger there,
> For thence may best his curious eye,
> The memorable field descry ;
>   And shepherd boys repair
> To seek the water-flag and rush,
> And rest them by the hazel bush,
>   And plait their garlands fair ;
> Nor dream they sit upon the grave,
> That holds the bones of Marmion brave.

Both hazel bush, water-flag, rush, and shepherd
boys, have all vanished before an Act of Parliament and the plough. Hence, however, you have
a full and wide view of the scenery of the battle to
Twizel-bridge and castle, where the English crossed
the Till. From Flodden ridge you may see, in
the direction of Millfield, Ford Castle, the seat of
the Herons, whose conquest was so fatal to James,

—now the property of the Marquis of Waterford. The features of the battle-field have been tamed down by the hand of cultivation; the open waste of "red Flodden" has given way to hedges; its heather to corn; and the very King's Chair itself is broken by the hammer and the pick; but the wooded ridge and the little well will not easily be annihilated; and many a ruin or site in the neighbourhood, connected with the field of Flodden, or with stirring passages in border warfare, render this a most delightful resort for a summer-day's party; especially of such as have hearts and imaginations to raise again the ruined ranks, and see as Scott saw, the last scene of that contest, when—

> On the darkening heath
> More desperate grew the strife of death,
> The English shafts in volleys hailed,
> In headlong charge their horse assailed;
> Front, flank, and rear, the squadrons sweep,
> To break the Scottish circle deep,
>   That fought around their king.
> But yet, though thick the shafts as snow,
> Though charging knights like whirlwinds go,
> Though bill-men ply the ghastly blow,
>   Unbroken was the ring.
> The stubborn spearmen still made good
> Their dark impenetrable wood,

Each stepping where his comrade stood,
    The instant that he fell.
No thought was there of dastard flight;
Linked in the sorried phalanx tight,
Groom fought like noble, squire like knight,
    As fearlessly and well;
Till utter darkness closed her wing
O'er their thin host, and wounded king.
Then skilful Surrey's sage commands
Led back from strife his shattered bands;
    And from the charge they drew;
As mountain waves from wasted lands
    Sweep back to ocean blue.
Then did their loss his foemen know;
Their king, their lords, their mightiest low,
They melted from the field as snow
When streams are swoln, and south winds blow,
    Dissolves in silent dew.
Tweed's echoes heard the ceaseless plash,
    While many a broken band,
Disordered, through her currents dash,
    To gain the Scottish land;
To town and tower, to down and dale,
To tell red Flodden's dismal tale
And raise the universal wail.
Tradition, legend, tune and song,
Shall many an age that wail prolong;
Still from the sire the son shall hear
Of the stern strife and carnage drear,
    Of Flodden's fatal field,
Where shivered was fair Scotland's spear,
    And broken was her shield.

The ballads and traditions of Scotland are full
of the lamentation and the desolation long produced there by this fatal battle.

"The Scots," says Sir Walter Scott, "were
much disposed to dispute the fact that James IV.
had fallen on Flodden Field. Some said he had
retired from the kingdom, and made a pilgrimage
to Jerusalem. Others pretended that, in the twi-
light, when the field was nigh ended, four tall
horsemen came into the field, having each a bunch
of straw on the point of their spears, as a token for
them to know each other by. They said these
men mounted the king on a dun hackney, and
that he was seen to cross the Tweed with them at
nightfall. Nobody pretended to say what they did
with him, but it was believed he was murdered in
Howe Castle; and I recollect about forty years
since, that there was a report that, in cleaning the
draw-well of that ruinous fortress, the workmen
found a skeleton wrapt in a bull's hide, and having
a belt of iron round the waist. There was, however, no truth in this rumour. It was the absence
of this belt of iron which the Scots founded upon
to prove that the body of James could not have
fallen into the hands of the English, since they
either had not that token to show, or did not produce it. But it is not unlikely that he would lay

aside such a cumbrous article of penance on a day of battle; or the English, when they despoiled his person, may have thrown it aside as of no value. The body which the English affirm to have been that of James, was found on the field by Lord Dacre, and carried by him to Berwick and presented to Surrey. Both of these lords knew James's person too well to be mistaken. The body was also acknowledged by his two favourite attendants, Sir William Scott, and Sir James Forman, who wept at beholding it."

The singular history of these remains, Stow, in his "Survey of London," 4to, p. 539, thus furnishes from his own knowledge. What a strange end for so proud and chivalrous a king, and what treatment from the hands of a brother-in-law—Henry VIII.— who certainly refused the body Christian burial!

"After the battle, the bodie of the same king being found, was closed in lead, and conveyed from thence to London, and to the monasterie of Sheyne in Surrey, where it remained for a time, in what order I am not certaine; but since the dissolution of that house, in the reygne of Edward the Sixt, Henry Grey, Duke of Suffolke, being lodged, and keeping house there, I have been shewed the same bodie so lapped in lead, close to the head and bodie, throwne into a waste room amongst the old timber, lead, and other rubble. Since the which time, workmen there for their foolish pleasure, hewed off his head; and Lancelot Young, master glazier to Queen Elizabeth, feelinge a sweet savour to come from thence, and yet the form remaining, with the hair of the head and beard red, brought it to *London* to his house in *Wood-street,* where (for a time) he kept it for the sweetness; but, in the end, caused the sexton of that church to bury it amongst other bones, taken out of their charnel."

21*

VISIT TO BOLTON PRIORY.

THE man of genius is often looked upon as a being that shuts himself up, and knows little of what is going on in the real world around him. He is supposed to live in a fairyland of his own creation—often a very barren and profitless one— full of all manner of enchantments and magical delusions. In reference to him, men of arts and sciences, the men of spinning-jennies and steam-engines—nay, the naturalists, and many other writers—talk of themselves as *practical* men. They often smile at the poet and the romance-writer, as men of the world affect to do, and say, —"O! a very clever, a very clever fellow indeed; but as ignorant of actual life as a child." But the poets and romancers of late have proved themselves both to be profitable fellows and practical ones. To say nothing of the vast sums coined from the brain of Scott and of Byron; look at the comfortable nest which Moore has feathered for himself. Very pretty sums he has fobbed now and then. See old George Crabbe going down to his parsonage with 3000*l.* in his saddle-bags at one time. Look at the poet's house at Keswick: it has a library in it which has cost a fortune; and the poet and the historian sits there now, what with salaries, pensions, *Quarterly Review* articles, and residuary legateeships, as no inconsiderable man of substance. There is that "old man eloquent" too, his neighbour at Rydal Mount, who, if he have not amassed a mount of gold on which to build his palace, has got a poet's bower on one of the most delicious little knolls in Europe, warmed by as much affection and domestic peace as ever crowned one man's hearth; and having no mark or *stamp* of poverty about it. Yes, and spite of *Edinburgh* and *Quarterly*, and a host of lower critics who echoed their owl-notes, his poetry is become *fashionable!* Only think of that—" The Idiot Boy" and " Betty Foy," " The Old Wanderer" in his worsted stockings, and " Michael" and " The Wagoner," become fashionable, so that every critic who knows no more of poetry than he did ten years ago, now cries " glorious! divine! inimitable!" at every new edition of his poems. Yes, and so they shall cry— for such is the ultimate triumph of general sense and taste over professional stupidity. His poetry is become golden in all senses; and if government only act in the matter of copyright as a British government ought to act,* it will flow on in a golden stream to his children's children, to the third and fourth—ay, to the fortieth and four-hundredth generation.

These are your dreamers and thriftless poets of the present days! But they are not merely the profitable, they are the really practical men too. We ask, where would your Watts and Boltons be, if it were not for them? Why, it is they—it is the men of poetical genius—who build your steam-boats and steam-coaches. The man of genius is not now merely a scrawler on paper, a writer of poems or of tales; but his pen has become a magician's wand—the most potent one that was ever wielded: and while other men think that he is merely inditing some pleasant lay, or matter for a winter evening's fireside, they who see farther into a millstone know that he is actually building ships and boats, steam-engines and steam-carriages; launching new and splendid packets; laying down railroads, and carrying them through mountain and forest; erecting inns, furnishing them with hosts, and guests, and waiters; spreading tables with

* Not, however, by passing Mr. Serjeant Talfourd's present bill, with its retrospective clause, to smooth the bristled manes of the booksellers.

every delicacy of the season—as witness, ye grouse
on many a heathery hill, ye herrings of Loch Fine,
and salmon of countless lochs, and rivers running
like silver from the mountains—spreading them for
thousands who run to and fro in the earth; not
merely increasing knowledge of one another, but
the good luck of landlords, and the employment of
whole troops of poor and deserving men. The
man of genius does this, and more: he creates joint-
stock companies, he invests large capitals, he makes
captains and stewards of steamers, clerks, coach-
men, and sailors—these, and many other creatures
after their kind, are of his creation. Does any one
doubt it ?—Why, Sir Walter Scott has done more
than this, of his single arm. See what he has done
for Scotland. See every summer, and all summer
long, what thousands pour into that beautiful country, exploring every valley, climbing every mountain, sailing on every frith and loch, and spreading
themselves and their money all through the land.
And what roads and steam-vessels, what cars and
coaches are prepared for them! what inns are
erected!—and yet not half enow—so rapidly does
the spirit of the poetical and picturesque spread—
so wonderfully do the numbers of its votaries
increase, seeking a little easement of their swollen
purses, a little outlet for all their taste and enthu-

siasm. No less than nine hundred persons, on a
daily average, pass through the single city of Glasgow, chiefly of this class of persons, set astir by
this great spirit which has of late years sprung up,
the work of our poets and romancers. In summer
all the inns are filled jam-full; trains of omnibuses,
or omnibi, are flying down to the Broomielaw every
hour, to discharge the contents of the inns into the
steamers, and return with the living cargoes of the
steamers to the inns. Every hour the bell of some
packet, bound to the Highlands, the Western Isles,
Ireland, Wales, and all such places, attractive as
the very land of the Genii to poetical imaginations, is heard ringing out its call to the picturesque
and pleasure-hunters; and that call is obeyed by
swarms of eager tourists, to the height of all human
astonishment.

And when did all this grow up?—" O," say the
mere mechanic heads, " why, when steam created
such facilities." Yes, since the steam of poetic
brains created them ! Where would your steam-
boats and your railroads have been leading us, do
you think, if Bishop Percy had not collected the
glorious ballads of nature and of heroism that were
scattered over Scotland and England—the leaves
of a new Sibyl, a million times more fateful and
pregnant with wonders than the old; if Bishop

Percy had not done this, and set on fire the kindred heads of Southey, of Wordsworth, and of
Scott; if the "Border Minstrelsy" had not been
gathered by Scott; if ballads and eclogues of a
new school, if poems full of a pensive beauty and
a pure love, had not been framed by Southey; if
Wordsworth had not—stricken, as he confesses, by
the mighty power of nature through this very
medium—gone wandering all over the mountains
of Cumberland, filling his heart with the life of the
hills, and the soul of the over-arching heavens, and
the peace or passion of human existence hidden in
glens and recesses where poets had ceased to look
for them;—if the last of these great men had not
come forth again in a fresh character, with metrical
romances, and with historical romances in prose,
pouring a new spirit through field and forest;
bringing down from the mountains of the north a
clan life, and race of fiery warriors, with their
pride, their superstitions, their bloody quarrels, their
magnanimity of mutual devotion and fatal loyalty,
such as we should otherwise never have known;
and, besides this, peopling mountain and glen,
palace and cottage, garrison and town, with a host
of characters which live and move before us, as if
they were not the offspring of a mortal brain, but
of the earth and the heavens themselves? I say,

where would these steamboats and railroads now
have been leading their passengers? Why, dully
enough, to the market—to purchase cottons and
printed calicoes in Glasgow, Paisley, and Manchester; ashes and indigo in Liverpool; teas, and
a thousand other things in London! They would
be going, not the pack-horse, but the railroad round
of dull and wearisome commerce, wearing out his
own soul by his over-drudgery; and, even of these,
there would not have been a tithe of the present
outgoers. But now, the soul which has been crushed
under the weight of daily duty, has felt a spark of
this great spirit, has felt an indefinable impulse,
which is, in fact, the nascent love of nature and
out-of-door liberty; and, in the summer months, the
weavers and spinners, the thumpers and bumpers,
the grinders and shearers, the slaves of the desk,
the warehouse, the bank, and the shop, leap up, and
issue forth—as bear witness Sir George Head—by
hundreds and by thousands, in all directions, for a
pleasure that their fathers, poor old fellows! never
dreamed of on the most auspicious night of their
lives. O boats, whether on canal or river, driven
by steam or drawn by horse! O ships, on loch, or
frith, or ocean propelled by engines of three-hun-
dred-horse-power! cabs and cars, omnibi and
stages, inns and lodging-houses, wayside rests and

fishing taverns, Tom-and-Jerries, Tillysues or Kid-
ley-Winks! bear ye witness to the tribes set on fire
by this Walter Scott, these poets, and even these
naturalists—Bewick, Walton, Gilbert White, and
that class of quiet agitators—tribes who have gone
forth, to scramble up hills and tumble down them, to
sport parasols amongst frightened sheep, and scream
on precipices that they may fall into the arms of
careful lovers; to eat beef-steaks, and drink ginger-
beer and soda-water, with open windows, and
under trees, in boats or in booths—bear witness, all
of you, in all quarters of these islands! Let us hear
no more about the poets not being *practical* men:
they are the men practical and promotive of public
wealth and activity; they are your true political
economists, your diffusers of the circulating medium; in fact, your ship-builders, house-builders;
smiths, black, white, or copper; your tailors and
clothiers; your very hosts, cads, waiters, and
grooms—for, to all these, they give not merely employment, but life and being itself.

And yet it is a curious fact, that the poets and
the mechanists struck out into a new and bolder
line together; that this new growth and outburst
of intellect and ideality—this *revival* in the world
of mind—indicated its presence at once in the ima-
ginative and the constructive crania. It is curious

that steam, mechanism, and poetry, should have been brought simultaneously to bear in so extraordinary a degree on the public spirit and character. The love of poetry and nature, of picturesque scenery and summer-wandering, no sooner were generated by the means I have here stated, than lo! steamers appeared at the quays, and railroads projected their iron lines over hill and dale. Impulse was given at the same moment to the public heart, and facility to yield to it. Had the one appeared without the other, there must have been felt a painful restraint, an uncomprehended but urgent want. Had the poetic spirit come alone, it would have lacked wings to fly to the mountains and the ocean shores. Had the mechanic impetus arisen without this, it would have wanted employment for its full energies. Their advent was coincident; and their present effect is amazing, and their future one a matter of wild speculation and wonder.

But there is yet another feature of this subject that is worthy of notice; and that is, how cunningly our great masters have gone to work. Call them dreaming and improvident! It is the most absurd abuse of language ever committed. There is no class of men more notorious for saving and care-taking than that of your great geniuses. Ac-

cordingly, as we go through the country, propelled
in the human tide by the double power of poetry
and steam, what is one of the first facts that seizes
on your attention? Why, the ingenuity and tact
with which these thoughtless poets and air-dreaming
romancers have laid hold, not only of the most glorious *subjects*, but the most glorious *scenes*. They
know that, next to a popular theme, is the popular
location of it—and what beautiful spot is there now,
from Land's-End to John-O'Groat's—what spot
known for its loveliness, or sacred for its history,
or made mysteriously interesting by traditions—on
which they have not seized? The monks were
said, of old, to have pounced upon all the para-
disaical valleys and rich nooks of the country; but
the poets have pounced upon them now. The
ancients were accused of having robbed us of all
our fine thoughts and spirit-stirring topics; but the
modern poets have taken away our very mountains
and battle-fields, our fairy haunts and our waters,
lying under the beautifying lights and shades of
love, and heroism, and sorrow. They have preoccupied them before our very eyes. There is
nothing which has impressed me so much with the
prescience and deep sagacity of our great modern
geniuses, as the care with which they have perched
themselves on every pleasant nook and knoll all

over the land. It reminds me, ludicrous as the
illustration is, of the nursery-tale of the young bears
that came into their house; and one said, " Who
has taken my fork?" and another, " Who has
eaten of my bread ?" and a third, " Who has sate
in my chair?" and another, " *Who is this sleeping
in my bed ?*"   Every spot of interest has this Scott,
this Wordsworth, or this Campbell appropriated
—and who does not admire their policy?   The
grandeur and intellectuality of a subject may, of
themselves, give it a great charm ; but it is better
to have two strings to your bow—a subject noble
and beautiful in itself, linked to noble and beautiful
scenery ; not confined to the library or the fireside book, but thrown, as it were, in the way of
the public, cast before the summer wanderers,
where natural beauty and traditional romance exert
a double influence.   What a fine effect it has, both
for poet and reader, when, as you stop to admire
some lovely landscape, some sublimity of mountain
or sea-shore, you hear it said—" This is the scenery of Marmion—this is the Castle of Ellangowan
—this is the spot where Helen M'Gregor gave her
celebrated breakfast—here fought Baillie Nicol
Jarvie with his red-hot ploughshare—this is Lam-
mermuir—or this is Artornish Hall."   What a
charm and a glory suddenly invest the place ! How

deep sinks the strain of the bard or the romancer
into your soul! The adroitness with which great
names have thus been written—not on perishable
paper, but on every rock and mountain of the land
—is admirable. To compare great things with
small—it is like the hand-writing on the wall, of
Warren, or of Mechi; it is seen everywhere, and
who shall possibly erase it from his mind? But,
admirable as the plan is, who shall now adopt it?
The day and the opportunity are past. Did the
same ability exist to inscribe places at once to the
glory of the poet and their own name, it is too
late; the field is preoccupied. The clan regions
and the Borders of Scotland—ground rife with
matter—are all Scott's, by right of discovery, and
by the mighty hand of the conqueror. If you go
to the isles—Shetland, Hebridean, or Orcadian—
he has been there too; and Campbell has there
placed his name, in Runic cipher, with that of
Reullura and the "dark-attired Culdee." Wordsworth is—

> Sole king of rocky Cumberland.

Scott, again, extends his influence over Durham,
Derbyshire, and Warwickshire; and southward,
tradition becomes more faint—all, at least, which

Shakspeare has not appropriated, and what he left to his proper heirs. We cannot, indeed, say what genius may yet draw from material which still lies unseen or unregarded—for its power is boundless; but, in the mean time, let us wander over a few spots of consecrated ground, and admire what has been done by " the giants that have been in the land."

SCENERY OF "THE WHITE DOE OF RYLSTON."

WE visited this scenery much in the order in which it is introduced to our notice in Wordsworth's poem. First, the White Doe is seen at Bolton Priory; then you have a glimpse of the history of the Shepherd Lord, and his residence, Barden Tower; lastly, the poet takes you to Rylston, and enters, with earnest heart, into the fate of the Nortons. We took the same course. We walked from Skipton Castle to Bolton Priory, on the morning of the 6th of July. The country had nothing very remarkable in it, if we except the wild aspect of Rumbold's Moor—a corruption of Romilley's Moor—on our left as we went; nothing

which bore any relation to that exquisite scenery
which we looked for in the neighbourhood of Bolton.   As we drew near, indeed, we could not help
saying repeatedly—" We fear we shall be disappointed in this place." Presently, however, a valley
filled with dense wood appeared below us, stretching away northwards.   We came to a few cottages
in their gardens, to a high stone wall ; and passing
through a small arched gateway, the valley and
ruins of Bolton Priory lay before us ; one of the
most delicious and paradisiacal scenes which the
heart of England holds.   The effect upon our spirits
was one of profound and soothing delight.   We
sate down on a rustic bench placed just within the
gateway, and contemplated it in silent enjoyment.
We were on a green elevation, somewhat above
the valley, and the scene lay before us in all its
loveliness; a vale in which all the charms of peaceful variety, which poetry delights to combine in
some fairy paradise, were concentrated.   It was a
splendid morning; and the freshness of the greensward, of the trees, the glittering dews, the cheerful
voices of birds, the profusion of blossoms around
on bush and bank, made the scene perfect.   There
were the gables and pinnacles of the Priory, appearing amongst a wilderness of trees in the open bosom
of the valley ; there was the Wharf, sounding on

his way with a most melancholy music, under the
cliffs opposite; there was the silver line of a waterfall, thrown from a cliff of considerable and nearly
perpendicular height, a cliff of rich purple hue,
facing the eastern end of the Priory; there were
the parsonage, and other houses shrouded in their
trees; beyond, lay the deep and densely-wooded
vale; on the northern slope above it, the ancient
oaks of the park; and still farther, the fells and
rocky distances of Barden and Simon-Seat. Whittaker, in his "History of Craven," says well that,
for picturesque effect, the site of this Bolton Priory
has no equal amongst the northern houses, and perhaps in England.

As we descended and walked towards the Priory,
the parsonage presented a very inviting aspect. Its
garden, crimson with roses; its old ivied porch, in
a sort of tower, with an ancient escutcheon emblazoned on it—I believe of the Clifford arms; its
pleasant shrubberies, and its little garden gateway
up a few steps, overhung, on each hand, with
drooping masses of yellow fumitory, made it one of
the most perfect little rural nests we ever set eyes
upon. As soon as we passed this, the Priory broke
upon us with a fine effect. We need not attempt
to describe it; it is a fit subject for the pencil only;
and the pencils of many of our artists, particularly

that of Turner, have made it familiar to the public eye. The magnificent ash-trees, however, which grew about, deserve especial mention. One, in particular, secured with iron hoops and stays from the effects of storms on its mighty limbs, showed that their beauty was felt and appreciated; and indeed, the ash about this place generally, has an extraordinary stateliness and grandeur of growth.

The nave of the Priory church is now used for a parochial chapel.

In the shattered fabric's heart
Remaineth one protected part—
A rural chapel, neatly drest,
In covert like a little nest;
And thither young and old repair
On Sabbath-day, for praise and prayer.

White Doe, p. 8.

But the most singular feature of this beautiful structure, is a tower, or western entrance, built like a screen before the old western entrance. This was begun by Prior Moore, the last prior before the dissolution, but never finished. It possesses a fine receding arch, and is embellished with shields, statues, and a window of exquisite tracery. Amongst others on this part of the work, is the

statue of a pilgrim, with a staff in one hand, and a
broad, flat, round hat in the other. The buttresses
are surmounted with figures of hounds. Within
this, partly darkened and partly hidden by it,
appears the old front, with its lancet windows and
slender columns—a work equally exquisite of its
kind. The sculpture and carvings of the Priory
altogether, its running trefoils and fleur-de-lis, have
preserved their sharpness and distinctness most remarkably.

Opposite to this western entrance stands the
Duke of Devonshire's house—a small castellated
building—a mere nut-shell to his other houses—
Chatsworth, Hardwicke, Chiswick, or Devonshire
House. In fact, it is formed out of the original
gateway of the Priory—the principal room being
the gateway itself, with walls run across it. It
serves, however, for a sporting-box, when his
Grace comes hither in autumn to the moors, and
contains a marvellous number of beds for its compass. The walls of the principal apartment are
adorned with pieces from classical subjects; with
horns of stags and antelopes, and with some paintings, the most interesting of which are, one of the
Boy of Egremond about to leap the Strid, with his
dog in a leash, and a puppy at the dog's heels—a
circumstance that I do not recollect as forming

part of the tradition. A portrait of Sir Philip Sidney, and a curious picture of the seven sons of one of the Earls of Burlington. There is one of the celebrated Earl and Countess of Derby ; some family portraits of the Cliffords and Burlingtons; and several of the Charleses and Jameses, and their queens—of little value.

But our attractions lay out of doors. We hastened down to the Wharf, and crossed it, by a row of stepping-stones, into the woods on the opposite side. These stones are solid square blocks of considerable size, and require some courage in the passer; for, though the river is not deep here, it is very rapid, clear, and broad, and rushes on with an awful sound, especially after heavy rains, as had been the case then ; so that the water flowed, in some places, over the stones. Immediately after us came across two young ladies, whom we found to be the clergyman's niece, Miss Kitty Crofts, and her young friend, Julia somebody. They had their rural dinner in a basket, and were going to spend the day in the woods. They accompanied us about a mile up through the woods, and very politely directed our attention to the striking points of the scenery, and gave us directions for our course to Barden Tower, which every now and then showed itself up the valley.

Nothing can exceed the beauty and delightful-
ness of these woods, which run on each side of the
sounding Wharf; and the public owes much to the
worthy clergyman, Mr. Carr, for having rendered
the forest banks of the Wharf accessible, opening
up the turns and reaches of the river, and the views
of the Priory downwards, and of Barden Tower
upwards, with the most admirable taste and effect.
All through the woods, for miles on each side, run
winding walks; and wherever seats are placed,
there you may be sure is some new view of
river, ruins, forest, or fell.   The woods themselves
afford a delicious retreat in the noon-blaze of a
summer's day; they present such sylvan seclusion;
such dark and shadowy nooks; such mossy slopes,
where spring throws out by thousands her prim-
roses, and summer her delicately-veined flowers
and green leaflets of the oxalis; such wildernesses
of heather and bilberry, of ferns and polypodies;
such dim chaos of craggy masses or uplifted gray
cliffs, hung with ivy and overshadowed with boughs.
But then, the river below!—such a dark brooding
stream at one place; such a wild hurrying torrent
at another, sending up its softened roar all through
the woods.   I never saw a stream that so vividly
brought before me the descriptions of rivers flowing through American forests, with their foamy

rapids, and their dark woodland steeps, and wild boughs overhanging the stream.

About a mile from the Priory we came to the celebratsd STRID—

> The pair hath reached that fearful chasm—
> How tempting to bestride!
> For lordly Wharf is there pent in,
> With rocks on either side.
>
> This striding-place is called THE STRID—
> A name it took of yore;
> A thousand years hath it borne that name,
> And shall a thousand more.
>
> And hither is young Romilly come;
> And what may now forbid
> That he, perhaps for the hundredth time
> Shall bound across THE STRID!
>
> He sprung in glee, for what cared he
> That the river was strong and the rocks were steep!
> But the greyhound in the leash hung back,
> And checked him in his leap.
>
> The boy is in the arms of Wharf,
> And strangled by a merciless force;
> For never more was young Romilly seen,
> Till he rose a lifeless corse.
>
> *The Force of Prayer. Wordsworth's Poems.*

The Strid is not so much a waterfall as a narrow

passage, torn by the river through its bed of solid
rock, through which it rushes with tremendous
fury and a stunning din. Many people, who go
expecting to see a sheer cascade, are at first disappointed; but no one can stand long by it without
feeling a sense of its power and savage grandeur
grow upon him. It is indeed a place " most tempt-
ing to bestride ;" and, notwithstanding the repeated
fatalities which have occurred there since that of
the boy Egremond—one of a young lady, in the
very presence of her lover, but a few years ago—I
felt an intense desire to take the leap, and should
have done so, had it not been for the earnest dissuasion of my companion. I am, however, very
sensible, that, narrow as the opening appears, its
real width is much greater than its apparent one ;
and very dangerous, both on that account, and
from the slipperiness of the rocks. One slip of the
foot, and the *leap* is into eternity.

As we stood here, we were delighted to see the
various parties that came up, or that were to be
seen glancing at intervals in the woods—gay young
spirits, full of the enjoyment of fresh life, of social
affection, and natural beauty ; another proof of the
manner in which all places of natural or historical
interest are now visited—the happy consequence of
the spirit of modern literature, and we were, per-

haps, most pleased with the sight of a party of Friends, in their dove-coloured robes and drab bonnets. If you cannot see them at places of *artificial amusement*, there are no people whom you now more frequently meet at places of *natural amusement*—a satisfactory evidence that the spirit of modern literature has extended itself to them too; that the Wiffens, the Bartons, the Stickneys, and other writers of the Society, are not exceptions, but merely indications of that love of poetry, polite literature, and the fine arts, which a puritanic zeal in some of its founders unhappily banished from it for a time.

We now advanced to Barden Tower, the walk thither being still up the valley along the banks of the Wharf, and through the most delightful scenery. The splendour of the day, and the beauty of the place, filled us with delight and admiration. We crossed a fine bridge to Barden, and soon stood before the ruined tower of the Cliffords.

It is a singular circumstance, out of what peaceful, profound, old-fashioned nooks, have gone forth some of the stormiest, sternest, and most ambitious characters in history. Whittaker says—" The shattered remains of Barden Tower stand shrouded in ancient woods, and backed by the purple distances of the highest fells. An antiquarian eye rests with pleasure on a scene of thatched houses and barns, which in the last two centuries have undergone as little change as the simple and pastoral manners of the inhabitants." The place, in fact, seems to belong to a past age of English history; to make no part of bustling, swarming, steam-engine, and railroad England; but of England in the days of solemn forests, far-off towns, and the most peaceful and rustic existence. The tower stands a mere shell; but the cottages about it are those which stood there in the days of its glory, and are peopled with a race as primitive and quiet as they were then. We inquired for a public-house to get a luncheon; there was no such thing; but we procured bread and butter, and milk, at one of the cottages; and, as we sate looking out of its door, the profound tranquillity of the scene was most impressive. It was a sultry and basking noon; around were lofty ancient woods; on the opposite slope a few cottages, half-buried in old orchards, and gardens with their rows of bee-hives; and an old man at work with his hoe, as slowly and as gravely as an object in a dream, or a hermit in his unpartaken seclusion. Yet from this place, and such as this issued

The stout Lord Cliffords that did fight in France,

ay, and in Scotland and England too—conspicuous
in all the wars, from the time of the Conqueror to
that of Cromwell; the "Old Clifford," and the
"Bloody Clifford," who slew the young Duke of
Rutland, and afterwards the Duke of York, his
father—of Shakspeare's "Henry VI." Thence,
too, went out the great seafaring Lord Clifford,
George, third Earl of Cumberland, of Elizabeth's
time, who made eleven expeditions, chiefly against
the Spaniards and Dutch, and chiefly too, at his
own expense, to the West Indies, Spanish America,
and Sierra Leone. But the most remarkable characters connected with this place are—the Shepherd Lord Clifford; the heroic Countess of Derby,
daughter of Henry, second Earl of Cumberland,
and grand-daughter of Charles Brandon, Duke of
Suffolk, and the Dowager Queen of France, sister
of Henry VIII., whose romantic story is known to
all readers of English history; and especially Anne
Clifford, Dowager Countess of Pembroke and Montgomery, of famous memory: for the others made
only occasional visits hither, from their more frequent residence of Skipton Castle, to enjoy field-
sports at their lodge here; but Anne Clifford has
placed her memorial on the very front of the house,
as its restorer; and the Shepherd Lord constituted
it his principal abode.

23*

Anne Clifford has justly been termed one of the most extraordinary women which this country has produced. - She was a woman of a high spirit, a determined will, and many good and magnificent qualities, and of a very commensurate consciousness of them. She did great works, and took good care to commemorate them. Two such builders of houses and of families, perhaps no nobleman of the present day can reckon amongst his female ancestry, as the Duke of Devonshire—Anne Clifford, and Bess of Hardwicke. The first thing which strikes your attention in front of Barden Tower, is this singular inscription :—

THIS BARDEN TOWER WAS REPAYRED
BY THE LADIE ARNE CLIFFORD COUNTE
SSE DOWAGER OF PEMROKEE DORSETT
AND MONTGOMERY BTRONESS CLIFFORD
WESTMERLAND AND VERCIE LADY OF THE
HONOR OF SKIPTON IN CRAVEN AND HIGH
SHERIFESSE BY INHERITANCE OF THE
COUNTIE OF WESTMERLAND IN THE YEARSS
1658 AND 1659 AFTER IT HAD LAYNE
RUINOUS EVER SINCE ABOUT 1589 WHEN
HER MOTHER THEN LAY IN ITT AND WAS
GREAT WITH CHILD WITH HER TILL
NOWE THAT IT WAS REPAYRED BY

THE SAID LADY.   IS. CHAPT. 58. V. 12.
GOD'S NAME BE PRAISED !

The text referred to is—" Thou shalt build up the
foundations of many generations, and thou shalt be
called the repairer of the breach, and the restorer
of paths to dwell in."

When she came to her ancestral estates, she
found six castles in ruins, and the church of Skipton
in a similar condition, from the ravages of the Civil
War. She restored them all ; and upon all set this
emblazonment of the fact. One of the first things
which she built, was a work of filial piety—a pillar
in the highway, at the place where she and her unhappy mother last parted, and took their final farewell. She erected monuments to her tutor, Daniell,
the poetic historian, and to Spenser—the latter in
Westminster Abbey. She wrote her own life—of
which the title-page is indeed a title-page, being a
whole page of the most vain-glorious enumeration
of the titles and honours derived from her ancestors.
Spite of her vain-glory, she was, nevertheless, a
fine old creature. She had been an independent
courtier in the court of Queen Elizabeth, possessing
a spirit as lofty and daring as old Bess herself.
She personally resisted a most iniquitous award of
her family property by King James, and suffered

grievously on that account. She rebuilt her dis-
mantled castles, in defiance of Cromwell; and re-
pelled with disdain the assumption of the minister
of Charles II. " She patronised," says her historian,
" the poets of her youth, and the distressed loyal-
ists of her maturer age; she enabled her aged
servants to end their days in ease and independence; and above all, she educated and portioned
the illegitimate children of her first husband, the
Earl of Dorset. Removing from castle to castle,
she diffused plenty and happiness around her, by
consuming on the spot the produce of her vast
domains, in hospitality and charity. Equally remote from the undistinguishing profusion of ancient
times and the parsimonious elegance of modern
habits, her house was a school for the young and a
retreat for the aged; an asylum for the persecuted;
a college for the learned; and a pattern for all."
To this it should be added, that, during that age
when such firmness was most meritorious, she with-
stood all the arts, persuasions, and all but actual
compulsion of her two husbands, to oblige her to
change the course and injure the property of her
descendants; and therefore, it must be confessed
that she was a brave woman, and one whose like
does not often appear. It is, however, her celebrated
letter to Sir Joseph Williamson, the secretary of

Charles II. who had written to name a candidate
for her borough of Appleby, that has given her
name a Spartan immortality :—

"I have been bullied by an usurper; I have
been neglected by a court; but I will not be dictated to by a subject—your man shan't stand.

ANNE, DORSET, PEMBROKE,
AND MONTGOMERY."

The history of the Shepherd Lord is one of the
most singular in the peerage. When his father,
Lord John Clifford—the bloody or black-faced
Clifford—fell at the battle of Towton, which over-
threw the house of Lancaster, and placed Edward
IV. on the throne, his mother was obliged to fly
with him, for safety, into the wildest recesses of
Yorksire and Cumberland. She afterwards married
Sir Launcelot Threlkeld, of the latter county, who
assisted to keep him concealed from the knowledge
of the York family—to whom the Clifford blood
was, for notorious reasons, most especially odious ;
but to effect this, he was obliged to be brought up
as a shepherd, and so lived for twenty-four years.
On the ascension of Henry VII. to the throne,
the attainder against his father was reversed, and
he succeeded to his ancestral honours and estates.

At this period, it appears that he was as unedu-
cated as his fellow shepherds; but he was a man of
strong natural understanding, and had, it would
seem, learned much true wisdom in his simple
abode up amongst the hills.

Among the shepherd-grooms no mate
Had he—a child of strength and state!
Yet lacked not friends for solemn glee,
And a cheerful company,
That learned of him submissive ways,
And comforted his private days.
To his side the fallow-deer
Came and rested without fear;
And both the undying fish that swim
Through Bowscale Tarn did wait on him—
The pair were servants of his eye,
In their immortality;
They moved about in open sight,
To and fro for his delight.
He knew the rocks which angels haunt
On the mountains visitant;
He hath kenned them taking wing;
And the caves where fairies sing
He hath entered; and been told,
By voices how men lived of old,
Among the heavens his eye can see
Face of thing that is to be:
And, if men report him right,
He could whisper words of might.

Wordsworth.

These verses allude to the studies for which he became remarkable; for he resorted to this Barden Tower, and put himself under the tuition of some of the monks of Bolton. With these he appears to have contracted a strong friendship, and to have passed a life of what must have been a very delightful prosecution of the popular studies of the time. They applied themselves to astronomy, and it seems equally certain, to *astrology*. In the archives of the Cliffords have been found manuscripts of this period, and supposed to belong to the Shepherd, which make it more than probable that *alchemy* was another of the fascinating pursuits of Lord Henry and his monkish companions. Some of these verses conclude with the usual declaration that the writer could not disclose the grand secret.

> Hie wer accursyde that soo wolde done.
> How schold yow have servans then,
> To tyll your lands, and dryffe your plughe?
> Yff ev'ry mane to ryches came,
> Then none for oth'r owght wolde dowghe.

There is matter for a fine romance in the life of this lord: the stirring nature of the times when he was born; the flight of his family; his concealment; his life on the mountains; his restoration;

his secluded mode of existence and mysterious la-
bours; and then his emerging, as he did, after he
had so spent the whole of the reign of Henry VII.
and the first years of Henry VIII., at the age of
nearly sixty, as a principal commander of the victorious army of Flodden; showing that the military
genius of the Cliffords merely slumbered beneath
the philosophic gown.   There is something very
picturesque in the description of his followers, in
the old metrical history of Flodden Field.

> From Penigent to Pendle Hill,
> From Linton to Long Addingham,
> And all that Craven coasts did till—
> They with the lusty Clifford came;
> All Staincliffe hundred went with him,
> With stripling strong from Wharlédale,
> And all that Hauton hills did climb,
> With Longstroth eke and Litton Dale,
> Whose milk-fed fellows, fleshy bred,
> Well-browned, with sounding bows upbend;
> All such as Horton Fells had fed—
> On Clifford's banner did attend.

Before leaving Barden Tower, we must just
notice the singular old chapel which bounds one
corner of the court-yard. You enter at a door
from the court, and find yourself in a dwelling-
house; another door is opened, and you find your-

self in the loft of a very old chapel, which remains in the state in which it was centuries ago, except for the effects of time, and where service is still performed by the clergyman of Bolton.

We now directed our course to Rylston; but hearing that the common way was circuitous, and being curious to pass along the very route of the White Doe, we determined to cross the moor, contrary to the earnest dissuasion of the villagers, who declared it was perfectly trackless, and that a stranger could not find his way over it. And sure enough we found it the most solitary and impracticable waste we ever traversed. The distance was six miles; not a track nor a house to be seen, except a keeper's lodge, standing in the brown heathery wilderness about a mile from Barden, with a watch-tower annexed to it, whence he might look out far and wide for depredators on the moor-game. We had the precaution to take a young man with us as guide, and on we went, plunging up to the waist in the heather, and sinking in deep moss at every step; now in danger of being swallowed up by a bog, and now put to our contrivances by some black ravine. A weary way of it the poor Doe must have had every Sunday from Rylston to Bolton Priory; and well, we thought, might the people deem it something supernatural.

Our guide himself found it no very easy matter to
steer his course aright, or to pursue it when he
thought it was right.   He directed his way by certain crags on the distant hill-tops, called the Lord's
Stones: and, when we gained the highest elevation,
whence we had immense prospect, we came to a
track cut through the moorland for the Duke to
ride along on his shooting excursions. He told us
to follow that, and it would lead us to the Fell-gate
just above Rylston.   Here, therefore, we allowed
him to return; but we speedily repented the per-
mission, for the track soon vanished, and before us
lay only wild craggy moors with intervening bogs,
which extended wider and wider as we went. The
moor-game, ever and anon, rose with loud cries
and whirring wings; the few sheep ran off as we
made our appearance; and we seemed only getting
farther and farther into a desolate region—

Where things that own not man's dominion dwell,
And mortal feet had ne'er or rarely been.

Knowing, however, that there was nothing for it
but pushing on to the extremity of the waste, bring
us whither it would, we hurried forward in spite of
weariness and bewilderment, and presently found
ourselves on a savage ridge of crags, from which

a wide prospect of green and champaign country
burst upon us, and the village of Rylston itself
lying at the foot of the steep descent before us.
We hastened down as well as we could, and proceeded towards the churchyard, knowing that near
it had stood Rylston Hall, the abode of the Nortons.
Here we soon found that all vestiges of the old
house were gone, and that a modern gentleman's
house was built upon the site.   The village lies on
the green and cultivated plain, just that sort of
country which has a most attractive aspect to a
grazier, but which the poet gives but one glance
at; it has nothing picturesque in its appearance:
a more common-place collection of houses can
scarcely be met with, though three or four of them
are, no doubt, the dwellings of wealthy people.
We found the tradition of the White Doe quite
current still amongst the peasantry, who soon
pointed out to us, on the moorland eminence
whence we had descended, Norton Tower, still
exactly answering the description by the historian
of Craven :—" Rylstone Fell yet exhibits a monument of the old warfare between the Nortons and
Cliffords.   On a point of very high ground, commanding an immense prospect, and protected by
two deep ravines, are the remains of a square
tower, expressly said by Dodsworth to have been

built by Richard Norton.   The walls are of strong
grout-work, about four feet thick.   It seems to
have been three stories high.   Breaches have been
industriously made in all sides, almost to the
ground, to render it untenable.   The place is
savagely wild, and admirably adapted to the site
of a watch-tower."   Here, no doubt, stout old
Richard Norton used to assemble his retainers, to
make their inroads into Barden Moor amongst the
Cliffords' deer, in which he delighted, and for
which he constructed, by help of natural crag, and
bog, and ravine, that famous, and, to the Cliffords,
most provoking pound, of which abundant traces
yeat appear.   Here too, as the poet has more than
hinted, he used to come and make merry.

High on a point of rugged ground,
Among the wastes of Rylstone Fell,
Above the loftiest ridge, a mound
Where foresters or shepherds dwell,
An edifice of warlike frame
Stands single, Norton Tower its name.
It fronts all quarters, and looks around
O'er path and road, and plain and dell,
Dark moor, and gleam of pool and stream,
Upon a prospect without bound.

The summit of this bleak ascent,
Though bleak, and bare, and seldom free,

As Pendle-hill or Pennygent,
From wind, or forest, or vaporous wet,
Had often heard the sound of glee,
When there the youthful Nortons met
To practise games and archery.
How proud and happy they !   The crowd
Of lookers-on how pleased and proud !
And from the scorching noontide sun,
From showers, or when the prize was won,
They to the watch-tower did repair—
Commodious pleasure-house !   And there
Would mirth run round with generous fare ;
And the stern old Lord of Rylstone Hall,
He was the proudest of them all.

White Doe.   Canto V.

If the village of Rylston has little in the aspect of
the present or remaining of the past, to draw the
feet of poetic wanderers to it—if Rylston Hall itself,
the hearth and home of the stout Nortons, be gone
—if all its gardens, walks, waters, and topiary-work
have vanished like a dream,—yet there still stands
that stern old tower, on those dark and frowning
fells, which will rear their black and storm-shattered
heads till the shock which commingles earth and
heaven.   There they stretch along the grim edge
of that region of moorland, glen and forest, river
and ruin, over which have passed the consecrating
influences of heroic spirits crushed ·by malignant

24*

destinies, of human hearts and hearths laid waste and desolate for èver; and over which, once more, the poet has thrown a new and indestructible enchantment.

In this beautiful poem, "The White Doe of Rylston," Wordsworth has shown how far he was capable of handling a romantic and historic subject; and nothing is more obvious than that, if he had chosen to select such subjects, rather than undeviatingly attempting to develope his own views of the real nature and compass of the province of poetry, he might much earlier have stepped into that popularity which he has now attained, and avoided the long reign of ridicule and abuse under which he lived. To say nothing of Peter Bell, the Wagoner, Betty Foy, and that class of subjects—a class, and so treated, that I am free to confess to be fair game for critics that love a little fun;—it is quite as true as it was ten years ago, that neither the simple pathos of his "Lyrical Ballads," nor the grave dignity and philosophy of his "Excursion," ever could or ever can be truly appreciated by the common run of readers. They can have no charms for those who delight in the literary dram-drinking of fashionable novels. You might just as well have expected a Persian to love Spartan broth; just as well expect a London epicure, with his gullet on

fire with curry and cayenne, to relish the girdle-
cake and milk of the shepherd's hut.   In this poem
he has enlisted more of those stirring elements of
historical action and national change, with all their
sequences of family disruptions and disastrous over-
throws, which, for the habitual story-monger, may
become a tolerable *substitute* for his ordinary stimu-
lus of tragic recital and piquant personalities; and
which the reader, of genuine passion and healthful
sensibilities, may yet combine with gentler causes
and their emotions into a whole of living and exalt-
ing influences.   He has beautifully woven into his
scheme every history or tradition floating about the
scene of action with which our nature sympathises.
The fate of the Boy of Egremont, the fortunes of
the Shepherd Lord, blend like soft and sunset hues
into the great picture of " THE RISING IN THE
NORTH," of which the outline is gloriously sketched
in the ancient ballad of that name; the imposing,
but ill-organized and ill-maintained attempt to put
down in England the growing power of Protestantism, and to restore the old religion.   Here is
material enough to quicken the pulse of every true
Briton; but we soon find the poet, amid the splendour of historic matter, fixing his eye upon a few
characters, towards whom he irresistibly draws
our hearts after him; resting finally on that high-

spirited old gentleman, Maister Richard Norton, and his family,—his nine sons and single daughter. In working out the characters and fate of these, he finds ample employment for that philosophic taste, and that delight in tracing the movements of our inner nature ; the power of our affections ; the contention between our principles and our interests; the developement of that highest pitch of mortal grandeur, the stern subjection of every hope, feeling and ambition, to the sole and sovereign sense of duty shed into the heart of man by the law of Christianity. We, accordingly, behold with admiration the brave Richard Norton, who had spent his days amid his sons and vassals in the festivities of the hall, the excitements of the chase, and of Border war, now coming forward in his silver hairs to cast all the fortunes of his house on a single and hazardous die. We behold with equal admiration the unhesitating devotion of his eight sons, and their manly beauty, as they surround him, as he takes in his hand the banner wrought by the fair fingers of his only daughter—that banner which displayed

The Cross,
And the five wounds our Lord did bear.

Old Ballad.

The group, at this moment, would form a noble picture.

They mustered their host at Wetherby—
Full sixteen thousand, fair to see,
The choicest warriors of the North!
But none, for beauty and for worth,
Like those eight sons, embosoming
Determined thoughts; who, in a ring,
Each with a lance erect and tall,
A falchion, and a buckler small,
Stood by their sire on Clifford Moor,
To guard the standard which he bore.
With feet that firmly pressed the ground
They stood, and girt their father round;
Such was his choice—no steed will he
Henceforth bestride;—triumphantly
He stood upon the grassy sod,
Trusting himself to the earth, and God.
There, sight to embolden and inspire!
Proud was the field of Sons and Sire;
Of him the most; and sooth to say,
No shape of man in all the array
So graced the sunshine of that day.
The monumental pomp of age
Was with this goodly personage;
A stature undepressed in size,
Unbent, which rather seemed to rise,
In open victory o'er the weight
Of seventy years, to higher height;

Magnific limbs of withered state;
A face to fear and venerate;
Eyes dark and strong; and on his head
Bright locks of silver hair, thick spread;
With a brown morion, half concealed,
Light as a hunter's of the field.
And thus, with girdle round his waist,
Wheron the banner-staff might rest
At need, he stood, advancing high
The glittering, floating pageantry.

Nothing, we think, for a moment, can be more beautiful and admirable; but the poet soon shows us a character and a devotion far higher, in Francis Norton, the eldest son, who singly opposes and attempts to dissaude his father and brothers from this enterprise; and is repulsed as a coward and a renegade by the indignant father and the silently contemptuous sons. The wise spirit and unflinching fortitude of this English Abdiel impress us with a respect and veneration that are not easy to be heightened; and yet they are heightened by finding Francis, instead of satisfying himself with having striven to dissaude—and that vainly—and quietly sitting down to wait the result, or feeling resentful of the rude repulse and wrongful imputations received from them, now showing that the devotion and nobility of his nature are of a far loftier stamp. He follows them unarmed, and, unmindful of their taunts or their suspicions, watches with patient endurance for that moment of reversed fortune which he is sure will come, and when he hopes to render assistance that may be accepted and available. That moment of reverse soon arrives; but the indignant father only heaps fresh and more trying scorn on his faithful son; and it is only when the vengeance of the offended law dooms the father and the sons in arms to perish in their blood, that the sleepless and affectionate attentions of Francis, to soothe, and serve, and comfort them, break down the barrier of thick prejudice from the old man's heart, and he sees and acknowledges the wisdom and magnanimity of his devoted son. Here one scarcely knows whether most to admire, the frank confession of the old warrior and the confidence he immediately places in Francis, or the filial piety with which, to gratify the mind of his dying father, Francis undertakes a task, hopeless, and fatal to himself. The following out of these great human impulses; the portraiture of this sublime character of Francis Norton, than which none in history or fiction is greater; and, besides this, the beautiful sketch of his sister, equally devoted, equally strong in principle, though not so comprehensive and commanding in intellect as her brother; she

Whose duty was to stand and wait;
In resignation to abide
The shock, AND FINALLY SECURE
O'ER PAIN AND GRIEF, A TRIUMPH SURE :—

these, altogether, were elements of heart and spirit,
of character and action, in which the soul of the
philosophical poet, who has sought to link fast to
our theory of metaphysics *the system of the affections,* was sure to revel ; although on one occasion
we saw him, strangely enough, as the author of
" Peter Bell," and of this poem, lay down a volume
of a contemporary, full of the same elements, and
actually of a most kindred nature, saying that he
could not read of " sin and sorrow, finding enough
of them in the world about him."   Notwithstanding
this paradoxical assertion, he has here, in his own
case cast over the sorrows of the Nortons a profound sympathy, and a golden glory over the Scenery of the White Doe of Rylston ; over Bolton
Priory ; the Vale of Wharf ; over Barden Tower
and Norton Tower, on the grim Rylston Fells—
which, as it drew us thither, shall draw thither
also, from generation to generation, other pilgrims
as devoted to the charms of nature, of poetry, of
history and tradition, as ourselves.

VISIT TO HAMPTON COURT.

A visit to Hampton Court Palace, is one of the bravest pleasures that a party of happy friends can promise themselves. Especially is it calculated to charm the thousands of pleasure-seekers from the dense and dusty vastness of London. It lies in a rich country; on the banks of the Thames,— there unmuddled by commerce, but flowing free and pure, amid the greenest meadows, scattered villas, and trees overhanging its clear waters, and adding to its glad aspect the richness of their beauty. From the swelling hills of Richmond, Esher, and St. George, the palace is seen standing aloft amid a wide sea of woodland foliage, like a little town in its extent. Its ample and delightful gardens, bounded by the splendid masses of its lime-tree avenues; its ancient courts, with all their historic recollections; its accumulated paintings, the Cartoons of Raphael themselves being part of them—all are thrown open to the leisurely and perfect enjoyment of the public. There is no royal palace in England, excepting Windsor, which, after all, is to be compared to it, and this is, as it should be, given up to the use and refreshment of the people. It is the first step towards the national appropriation of public property. It is long since it was said, " The king has got his own again," and it is now fitting that the people should have their own again. Of all the palaces, the towers, the abbeys, and cathedrals, which have been raised with the wealth and ostensibly for the benefit of the people, none till lately have been freely open to the footsteps of the multitude. They have been jealously retained for the enjoyment of an exclusive few, or have been made engines to extort still further payment from those out of whose pockets they were raised. But the tolls at the door of St. Paul's and the Tower have been relaxed; park after park in the metropolis has been thrown open; and now this charming old palace of Hampton Court has been made the daily resort of any, and of all, of the English people who choose to tread the pavements, and disport themselves in the gardens, and gaze on the works of art, which for ages were wont only to be accessible to the royal, the aristocratic, and the ecclesiastical dignitary and their retainers.

These are visible and unequivocal evidences of

the growth of general intelligence, and of that
popular influence and benefit which must spring
out of it. Courts are no longer despotic because
the people is no longer ignorant. The crown has
resigned its lands into the hands of the people, saying, give us what you deem fitting for the just
maintenance of the regal dignity,—and the crown
has had no cause to regret this surrender; while,
on the other hand, it has given the people a right
to use a bolder tone regarding those which were
the royal lands and houses, woods and forests.
The people can now say with an air of just authority, we demand to be admitted to the use and
fruition of that for which we have given a noble
equivalent. It is with this consciousness that we
now walk about the courts, the gardens, the galleries, and painted chambers of Hampton Court;
and there can be perhaps no instance cited where
public property is more completely enjoyed by all
classes of the community. The royal race have
had their will of it from the days in which the last
great English Cardinal built it, and presented it, as
a most magnificent gift, to Harry VIII. his master,
till they abandoned it as an abode, for others which
more engaged their fancies. A considerable portion of it has since, and still is, given as residences
to branches of the aristocracy, and lo! at length

the very people have entered into possession of the
rest.

And now, the great question is, how do they enjoy it?—How do they use their advantage? Do
they feel the great delight of having got their own
again? Do they act like rational masters and proprietors on their own estates, committing no injury
and seeing none committed? A few facts will sufficiently answer these questions. Steam has in a
great measure brought this delightful old palace into the very suburbs of London; and thrown it open
to the thousands of its citizens. The Southampton
railway, passing within a short distance of it, has
enabled almost all that please to be down at it in
about an hour, and has given them a pleasant excursion at a cheap rate, through a delightful country, besides the luxury of fair gardens, on the
banks of the Thames, and the contemplation of
rich paintings when they get there. Have they
availed themselves of these privileges? The palace
has only been fairly thrown open this summer, and
for some time the fact was but very little known—
yet through spring and summer the resort thither
has been constantly increasing; the average number of visiters on Sunday or Monday is now two
thousand five hundred, and the amount of them for
the month of August was thirty-two thousand?

And how have these swarms of Londoners of all
classes behaved? With the exception of some
scratches made on the panels of the grand staircase, for the discovery of the perpetrator of which
an ominous placard is pasted on the door-post as
you enter, offering five pounds reward, but of
which slight injury no one can tell the date—the
police, who are always on the spot, never having
witnessed the doings of it since they were stationed
there—I cannot learn that the slightest exhibition
of what has been considered the English love of
demolition, has been made. Never have I seen, at
all times that I have been there, a more orderly or
more well-pleased throng of people. I happened
accidentally to be there on Whit-Monday, when,
besides the railway, upwards of a dozen spring-
vans, gaily adorned with ribbons, and blue and red
hangings, had brought there their loads of servants
and artisans, all with their sweethearts, and in fine
spirits for a day's country frolic; and not less than
two thousand people were wandering through the
house and gardens, yet nothing could be more
decorous than their behaviour. Never, indeed, did
I behold a scene which was more beautiful in my
eyes, or which more sensibly affected me. Here
were thousands of those whose fathers would have
far preferred the brutal amusement of the bull-bait-

25*

ing or the cock-pit; who have made holiday at the boxing-ring, or in guzzling beer in the lowest dens of debauch,—here were they, scattered in companies, and in family groups; fathers, mothers, brothers and sisters, old people and children of all ages, strolling through the airy gardens, admiring the flowers, or resting on the benches, or watching swarming shoals of gold and silver fish in the basin of the central fountain, and feeding them with crumbs of bun amid shouts of childish delight. Here were these poor people, set free from the fret and fume, the dust and sweat, and mental and bodily wear and tear of their city trades and domestic cares, well dressed, amongst their more wealthy neighbours, clean, and jocund from the sense of freedom and social affection, treading walks laid down only for royal feet, listening to the lapse of waters intended only for the ears of greatness and high-born beauty, though all constructed by the money of their forefathers; and here were they enjoying all these more than king or cardinal ever could do, beneath a sunny sky, that seemed to smile upon them as if itself rejoiced at the sight of so much happiness. There too, through the open windows, you saw the passing crowds of heads of men and women wandering through the rooms intent on the works of Raphael, Titian, Correggio,

Lely, Vandyke, Kneller, Rembrandt, Rubens, Ricci, Giulio Romano, and many another master of the sublime and beautiful; pausing to behold forms of power, and grace, and loveliness, and to mark many a face of man or woman whose names are so bruited in our annals that even the most ignorant must have heard something of them. Here surely was significant indication of a change in the popular mind in the course of one generation, which must furnish an answer to those who ask what has education done for the masses, and most pregnant with matter of buoyant augury for the future. Those who do not see in such a spectacle that the march of intellect, and the walking abroad of the schoolmaster, are something more than things to furnish a joke or a witticism, and blind indeed to the signs of the times, and to the certainty that the speed of sound knowledge amongst the people will yet make this nation more deserving of the epithet of a nation of princes, than ever Rome deserved from the Parthian ambassador. I could not help asking myself, as my eye wandered amid the throng, how much more happiness was now enjoyed in any one day on that ground, than had been enjoyed in a twelvemonth when it was only the resort of kings and nobles, and the scene of most costly masks and banquets. Nothing more

than the sight of that happiness was needed, to
prove the rationalty of throwing open such places
to diffuse amongst the million, at once the truest
pleasure and the most refining influences.

To the visiters of cultivated taste and historic
knowledge, Hampton Court abounds with subjects
of reflective interest of the highest order. It is
true, that, compared with some of our palaces it
can lay no claims to antiquity; but from the days
of Henry VIII. to those of George III., there are
few of them that have witnessed more singular or
momentous events.

Overbearing despot as Wolsey was, there is
something magnificent in the sweep of his ambition,
and irresistibly interesting in the greatness of his
fall. He was the last of those haughty prelates in
the good old Catholic times, rose up from the dust
of insignificance into the most lordly and overgrown magnificence; outdoing monarchs in the
number of their servants, and in the pomp of their
state. Equalling the great Cardinals who have
figured on the continent, Ximenes, Richlieu, Maza-
rine, and De Retz, in political ability and personal
ambition, he exceeded all in the wealth which he
unhesitatingly seized, and the princely splendour in
which he lived. He fell only just before, and
almost with, the Catholic religion itself in this coun-

try, and has therefore left a more marked place in men's memories. There could be none come after him of a like kind. Those swelling and mighty archprelates, filling the public ways with their enormous travelling processions, and ruling both as spiritual and temporal lords equally church and state, at once the primates and the prime ministers of the realm, could no more exist. Wolsey seemed to have gathered into himself all the powers and splendours of that extraordinary class of men, to have raised them to the highest pitch, to the uttermost blaze of exhibition, and to have quenched them in his fall. Never was such a rise, such a progress; such a sudden, sheer, and ruinous descent! It may be said that the Romish hierarchy fell with him, for nothing is more clear than that by first leading Henry to question the propriety of his marriage with Catherine of Arragon, in order to make way for a French alliance, which then appeared to him the surer way to the popedom, he opened the path of that royal license which led Henry into so much matrimonial villany and blood, and placed on the throne his enemy, and the enemy of popery, Anne Boleyn. He involved his irascible monarch in those terms with the Pope, which led him to kick down his power in this kingdom; and moreover, he was the first to lead the way to

the suppression of the monasteries, by showing to
Henry their enormous wealth and their profligate
state, that he might obtain from him an order for
the extinction of the worst, and appropriation of
their revenues to the building and endowing of his
colleges.

When we enter, therefore, the gates of Hampton
Court, and are struck with the magnificent extent
of the erection, which at that time not only,
according to Rapin, " was a stately palace, and
outshined all the king's houses," but was one of
the most splendid structures in Europe, we cannot help figuring to ourselves the proud Cardinal
surveying its progress, and musing over the wonders of that career which had brought him, if not
from the humble estate of the son of a butcher, yet
from an origin of no great condition, or it could
not have remained dubious to this period—the weal-
thiest man in Europe, the most potent in political
influence, and the ardent aspirant to the popedom
itself.   It would be curious to run over the multitude of offices and dignities, civil and ecclesiastical,
which this able adventurer had grasped in a daring
and rapid succession.   First, in 1504, chaplain to
King Henry VII., with dispensation to hold three
livings; then royal almoner; immediately afterwards, in 1508, Dean of Lincoln; in the next year,

Prebendary of Stowe Magna; in the autumn of the same year, 1509, made almoner to Henry VIII., with a grant of all goods and chattels of *felones de se*, and all coroners' deodands, which, although expressly reserving the whole proceeds of the offices to charitable purposes, no doubt were found very profitable in such hands. Next came the appointment of reporter of the proceedings in the Star Chamber, with acknowledged abundance of bribes for his good services with the king, in whose favour he already stood high.

In January, 1510, he received a formal grant of the parsonage and tenements of St. Bride's, with various gardens and other property, given him some time before; in February following he was appointed Canon of Windsor; in the same year he received the rich rectory of Turnington in the diocese of Exeter; and was made a privy councillor. Early in 1511 he was appointed Registrar of the order of the Garter; in February 1512, Dean of York; soon after, Prebend of Bugthorpe; in October, Dean of St. Stephen's, Westminster, now the House of Commons. In November of that year he was specially appointed to superintend the king's household and the preparation of the army for the invasion of France; and in September of the following year he was made Bishop of Tournay in that king-

dom. On the first of January, 1514, he became
Bishop of Lincoln; soon after he was elected
Chancellor of the University of Cambridge, but de-
clined the office; in June of that year the king
granted him half the advowson, or next reversion,
of Bermondsey Abbey, a valuable gift; and before
the year was out, he was actually on the throne
of the Archbishopric of York. The next year had
not passed over before he received from Rome a
cardinal's hat, and the appointment of Legate, and
from his king the seals of the office of Lord High
Chancellor of England. While honours and emolu-
ments thus showered upon him, Wolsey did not
hesitate to receive gifts and pensions from foreign
potentates. From the King of Spain, about this
time, he accepted a pension of 3000 livres per
annum, and another of 200 ducats from the Duke
of Milan. Then came a bull from the Pope, grant-
ing authority of visiting the monasteries, and con-
ferring on him the tenth of all the revenues of the
clergy. In 1518 the king empowered him to confer
letters patent of denizen under the great seal; and
then to make out *congés d'elire*, royal assents, and
restitutions of temporalities of ecclesiastical dignities, from archbishops down to the lowest religious
establishments; as well as to take the homages and
fealty of all persons which might be due to the

crown for such temporalities—sources of most extraordinary influence and emolument. Next was added the Bishopric of Bath and Wells, and the rich Abbey of St. Albans; then the administration of the sees of Worcester and Hereford was conferred on him by the Pope. In October of that year he received the grant of the office of Bailiff of the lordship of Cheshunt, in Hertfordshire, and parkkeeper of Brantingisley. In 1521 the Pope sent him a bull empowering him to make fifty knights, fifty counts palatine, forty apostolic notaries—whose privileges were equal to those made by the Pope himself, namely, to legitimate bastards—and confer degrees in arts, law, medicine, and divinity, and also to grant all sorts of dispensations. This was followed by another bull, empowering him to check and put down the new Protestant heresies. This year he was sent as ambassador to the king of France and the Emperor Charles V., and he received a grant of 9000 crowns of pension from the emperor, besides 2500 in lieu of a former grant of revenue out of the bishopric of Badajoz.

In 1522 he made himself master of the see of Durham—so rich that his predecessor had died that year worth 100,000l. In 1524 he received a new bull, confirming his power to visit and suppress disorderly monasteries; and in 1529, the

grant of the see of Winchester.   This was his last
favour, and came only about a year before his death.
When we add to all this, various grants of lands
and manors which have not been particularized,
and the many costly gifts and bribes received from
both crowned heads and numberless private persons to propitiate his favour in his days of palmy
fortune, we sum up an account of honour, prefer-
ment, and emolument, which had been growing,
with scarcely any intermission, through five-and-
twenty years.   Well might it be said, that the revenues in his command much exceeded the revenues
of the king, or indeed of any crowned head in Europe.   He exercised the powers, and was virtually
Pope in England.   The king seemed to delight in
showering upon him the most unbounded affluence,
and in seeing him expend the princely revenues derived from strictly national sources, on colleges
and palaces, to perpetuate the glory of his own
name.   This was the most magnificent portion of
the Cardinal's ambition.   He was ever emulous to
build up his fame with the advancement of learning.   He was the steady friend of Erasmus, and
the most learned men of the age.   He was the pro-
moter of what was called the " new learning," the
study of Greek ; he suggested the establishment of
the College of Physicians ; at his instigation Henry

invited both Titian and Raphael into England; he
established seven lectures at Oxford; commenced
a college at Ipswich, and founded, and nearly completed that of Christ Church Oxford, before his fall.
He appeared as enthusiastic and as superb in his
love of building, as he did in his ambition of power.
Wherever he was, he was busily employed in
building, and his structures are everywhere remarkable for their superiority to the general style
of the age. The greater part of them are of brick-
work, but that is of the most admirable and compact kind; and many of his fabrics still standing,
look comparatively new, and likely to endure yet
for ages. Besides Hampton Court, he restored and
enlarged his archiepiscopal house in York Place;
during his holding the see of Durham he built one-
third of the bridge over the Tyne; he built con-
siderably at Cheshunt, and at More in Hertfordshire, at the latter place inclosing with a wall
several hundred acres of additional park; and at
his house at Battersea. Esher Place, then the property of the see of Winchester, fell only into his
hands a short time before his disgrace, nevertheless, he is said to have repaired it, and built a new
gate-house, which is yet standing, though the house
itself, originally built by Bishop Waynflete, has
been pulled down some years.

At Apscourt, near Moulsey in Surrey, there is
the remains of a house said to have been built by
him, and to derive its name from A. P. S., the sign-
letters of Archiepiscopus: near Walton also, the
old mansion of Ashley Park is attributed to him ;
and even in his last days of trouble and disgrace,
on his melancholy journey to York, on arriving at
Cawood Castle, a palace of the archbishopric,
about seven miles from that city, where it was necessary to take up his abode, and finding it much
out of repair, he set about immediately to restore it.
He did it in his usual admirable manner; added
new buildings to it on a noble scale, and poor as
he then comparatively was, kept upwards of three
hundred workmen daily employed upon it.

Such was Wolsey when he built the Palace of
Hampton Court.   The actual ruler of this country,
both in church and state, by the unlimited favour
of his sovereign, and the courtesy of the Pope ;
flattered and sought by power and beauty at home,
and by the crowned heads of all Europe ; hated,
yet feared by the courtiers; haughty, arbitrary and
vindictive; possessed of revenues to which the in-
comes of the greatest nobles were poor, he lived in
a splendour and state such as became only a reign-
ing prince, and expressed his swelling vanity in the
well known words—Ego et Rex meus.   It was

only at Hampton Court that his vast train of servants and attendants, with the nobility and ambassadors who flocked about him, could be fully entertained. These, as we learn from his gentleman-usher, Cavendish, were little short of a thousand persons; for there were upon his " cheine roll" eight hundred persons belonging to his household, independent of suitors, who were all entertained in the hall. In this hall he had daily spread three tables. At the head of the first presided a priest, as steward; at that of the second a knight, as treasurer; and at the third his comptroller, who was an esquire. Besides these, there were always a doctor, a confessor, two almoners, three marshals, three ushers of the hall, and grooms. The furnishing of these tables required a proportionate kitchen: and there were two clerks, a comptroller, and surveyor of the dressers; a clerk of the spicery; two cooks, with labourers and children for assistants; turnspits a dozen; four scullery-men; two yeomen of the pastry, and two paste-layers. In his own kitchen was his master-cook, daily dressed in velvet or satin, and wearing a gold chain. Under him were two other cooks and their six labourers; in the larder a yeoman and groom; in the scullery a yeoman and two grooms; in the ewry two yeomen and two grooms; in the buttery

26*

the same; in the cellar three yeomen and three pages; in the chandlery and the wafery, each two yeomen; in the wardrobe the master of the wardrobe and twenty assistants; in the laundry, yeoman, groom, thirteen pages, two yeoman-purveyors and groom-purveyor; in the bake-house, two yeomen and two grooms; in the wood-yard one yeoman and groom; in the barn a yeoman; at the gate two yeomen and two grooms; a yeoman of his barge; the master of his horse; a clerk and groom of the stables; the farrier; the yeoman of the stirrup; a maltlour and sixteen grooms, each keeping four horses.

There were the dean and sub-dean of his chapel; the repeater of the choir; the gospeler, the epistler, or the singing priest; the master of the singers, with his men and children. In the vestry were a yeoman and two grooms. In the procession were commonly seen forty priests, all in rich copes and other vestments of white satin, or scarlet, or crimsom. The altar was covered with massy plate, and blazed with jewels and precious stones. But if such were his general establishment, not less was the array of those who attended on his person. In his privy chamber he had his chief chamberlain, vice-chamberlain, and two gentlemen-ushers. Six gentlemen-waiters and twelve yeomen; and at their

head nine or ten lords to attend on him, each with
their two or three servants, and some more, to wait
on them, the Earl of Derby having five. Three
gentlemen cup-bearers, gentlemen-carvers, and ser-
vers to the amount of forty in the great and the
privy chamber; six gentlemen-ushers and eight
grooms. Attending on his table were twelve
doctors and chaplains, clerk of the closet, two
clerks of the signet, four counsellors learned in the
law, and two secretaries.

He had his riding-clerk; clerk of the crown;
clerk of the hamper and chaffer; clerk of the
cheque for the chaplains; clerk for the yeomen of
the chamber; and "fourteen footmen garnished
with rich running-coates, whensoever he had any
journey;" besides these, a herald-at-arms, serjeant-
at-arms, a physician, an apothecary, four min-
strels, a keeper of the tents, an armourer; an
instructor of his wards in chancery; "an instructor of his wardrop of roabes;" a keeper of his
chamber; a surveyor of York, and clerk of the
green cloth.

"All these were daily attending, downelying and
uprising. And, at need, he had eight continual
boords for the chamberlaynes and gentlemen-offi-
cers, having a mease of young lordes, and another
of gentlemen; besides these, there never was a

gentleman or officer, or other worthy person, but he kept some two, some three persons to wait on them."

This was his state at home.   When he prepared to attend term at Westminster Hall, he summoned his retinue in his privy chamber, where he was ready appareled in his cardinal's robes; his upper vesture entirely of red, scarlet, or fine crimson taffeta, or crimson satin ingrained; his pillion scarlet, with a sable tippet about his neck.   He had in his hand an orange, which, having the inside taken out, was refilled with a sponge and aromatic vinegar, lest in the crowd he might imbibe any pestilence.   Before him were carried the great seal of England, and the cardinal's hat, by some "lord or gentleman, right solemnly."   On entering his presence chamber his two great crosses were borne before him, and the gentlemen-ushers cried, "On, masters, on, and make room for my lord."   On descending to the hall of his palace, he was preceded by additional officers, a serjeant-at-arms with a great silver mace, and two gentle-men bearing great plates of silver.   Arriving at his gate, he mounted his mule, trapped all in crimson velvet, with a saddle of the same, and thus he proceeded to Westminster—

Poleaxe and pillar borne before his face.—*Moile.*

his cross-bearers, and pillar-bearers all upon great horses, and in fine scarlet, with a train of gentry, footmen with battleaxes, etc.

Regularly on Sundays, when Henry held his court at Greenwich, which was often, the great lord cardinal made thither his progress to visit him. He had then his magnificent state barge, with troops of yeomen standing upon the sails, and crowds of gentlemen within and without. He disembarked to avoid the fall at London Bridge, and there his mule and cavalcade awaited him, to conduct him from the Three-Cranes of Billingsgate, where he again went on board; and the same solemn state was observed on his return.

When he celebrated mass before the royal family, the most distinguished noblemen held the basin for him to wash his hands: nay, when he performed mass at St. Paul's before Henry and Charles V. on his visit to this country, two barons gave him water before mass; two earls after the gospel; and at the last lavatory this office was performed by two dukes. The very Spaniards themselves who accompanied the emperor, are said to have been offended by his unparalleled assumption of dignity.

The whole establishment and style of life of Wolsey, however, more resemble the gorgeous

romance of an Arabian tale than any thing which
ever existed in the sober realm of England. His
friend and servant Cavendish relates scenes of
gaiety and revelry enacted within these very walls,
which it is sorrowful not to be able to give at
length here. " The cardinal's house," he observes,
" was resorted to like a king's house, by noblemen
and gentlemen, and such pleasures were here de-
vised for the king's delight as could be invented or
imagined. Banquets set with masquers and mum-
mers, in such costly manner, that it was glorious to
behold. There wanted no damsels meet to dance
with the masquers, or to garnish the place for the
time with variety of other pastimes. Then there
were divers kinds of music, and many choice men
and women singers appointed to sing, who had
excellent voices. I have seen the king come suddenly thither in a masque, with a dozen masquers,
all in garments like shepherds, made of fine cloth of
gold and silver wire, and six torch-bearers, besides
their drummers, and others attending on them with
vizards, and clothed all in satin : and before his
entering in the hall, you shall understand that he
came by water to the water-gate without any noise,
where were laid divers chambers and guns charged
with shot, and at his landing they were discharged,
which made such a rattling noise in the air, that it

was like thunder. It made all the noblemen, gentlemen, and ladies to muse what it should mean, coming so suddenly, they sitting quietly at a banquet. In short you shall understand, that the tables were set in the Chamber of Presence around, and my lord cardinal sitting under his cloth of state, and there having all his service alone; and then there were set a lady and a nobleman, a gentleman and a gentlewoman, throughout all the tables in the chamber on the one side, which were made all joining, as it were but one table. All which was done by my Lord Sands, then lord-chamberlain to the king, and by Sir Henry Guilford, then comptroller of the king's house.

" Then immediately after this great shot of guns, the Cardinal desired the Lord Chamberlain to see what it did mean, as though he knew nothing of the matter. They then looked out of the window into the Thames, and returning again told him, that they thought they were noblemen and strangers arrived at the bridge, and coming as ambassadors from some foreign prince; with that said the Cardinal, 'I desire you, because you can speak French, to take the pains to go into the hall, there to receive them into the chamber, where they shall see us, and all these noble personages, being merry at our banquet, desiring them to sit down with us, and take part of our fare.' "

So they are introduced, salute severally the Cardinal, declare the cause of their coming to be the rumour of such a constellation of beauty there that night; they beg to have a game at *mum-chance* with the ladies, which is accorded; and the Cardinal sends a message to them to the purport, that he believes there is amongst them a noble person who deserves the seat of honour at the feast more than himself, and begs that he will take it. They reply there is such a person, who if his grace can point him out, is willing to take his place most willingly. Wolsey pitches on his man, which turns out to be the wrong one; at which Bluff Harry pulls down his masque, and is very merry at the mistake. He goes and puts on a fresh and splendid dress, as do all his followers; a new banquet is laid, and they feast and dance till daylight.

This, it will be seen, is the masque given by Shakspeare in Henry VIII., but as occurring at York House, and with some difference of circumstance. A brief extract, from an entertainment given to the French ambassadors, will serve to show more completely the sort of scenes passing here in the palmy days of Wolsey. The king commanding the cardinal to entertain these gentlemen, orders were sent out to all of the carriers, purveyors, and other persons to prepare. The cooks wrought both day and night in many curious devices, when was no lack of gold, silver, or any costly thing. The yeomen and grooms of his wardrobes were busied in hanging the chambers with costly hangings, and furnishing the same with beds of silk, and other furniture of the same in every degree. . . . Then wrought joiners, carpenters, painters, and all other artificers needful, that there was nothing wanting to adorn this noble feast. There was carriage and re-carriage of plate, stuff, and other rich implements, so that there was nothing lacking that could be desired or imagined for that purpose. There were also provided two hundred and eighty beds, and all manner of furniture to them.

The Frenchmen were ready before their time, so they were taken to Hanworth, a park of the king's about three miles from Hampton, to hunt till night; when they were conducted to the palace, and all taken to their several chambers, where they found good fires, and stores of wine to entertain them till supper-time. They supped in the Great Waiting Chamber and Chamber of Presence, which were hung with rich arras, and furnished with tall

yeomen and goodly gentlemen, to serve. The
tables were set round the chambers, banquetwise,
covered. In the Waiting Chamber was a cupboard
garnished with white plate; and four great plates
were set with great lights, to give the more brilliancy, and a great fire of wood and coals. In the
midst of the Chamber of Presence was placed the
high table beneath the cloth of state, with six desks
of plate garnished all over with fine gold. The
cupboard was barred about that no man could
come very near it, for there were divers pieces of
great store of plate to use; besides the plates that
hung on the walls to give light, which were of
silver gilt, with wax-lights.

The trumpets blew, and the guests were conducted to the table; where, says Cavendish, " the
service came up in such abundance, both costly
and full of devices, with such a pleasant noise of
music, that the Frenchmen, as it seemed, were
wrapped up in a heavenly paradise."

The Cardinal was not there; but, at the second
course, he " came in, booted and spurred, suddenly
amongst them ; at whose coming there was great
joy, every man rising from his place." But my
Lord Cardinal made them all be seated, and being
in his riding apparel, called for his chair, and sate
him down in the midst of the high table, and was

there as merry and pleasant as ever I saw him in all my life.

" Presently after came up the second course, which was above a hundred several devices, which were so goodly and costly that I think the Frenchmen never saw the like. But the rarest curiosity of all the rest,'they all wondered at (which indeed was worthy of wonder) was a castle and images in the same, like St. Paul's church for the model of it. There were beasts, birds, fowls,—personages most excellently made ; some fighting with swords, some with guns, others with cross-bows ; some dancing with ladies, some on horseback in complete armour, justling with long and sharp spears, with many more strange devices. Among others, I noted there was a chess-board made of spice-plate, with men of the same, and good proportion. And because the Frenchmen are very expert at that sport, my Lord Cardinal gave that to a French gentleman, commanding that there should be made a good case, to convey the same into his country.

" Then called my lord for a great bowl of gold, filled with hippocras, and putting off his cap, said, ' I drink a health to the king my sovereign lord, and next unto the king, your master ;' and when he had drank a hearty draught, he desired the grand master to pledge him a cup, which cup was worth

five hundred marks, and so all the lords in order
pledged these great princes.   Then went the cup
merrily about, so that many Frenchmen were led
to their beds.   Then went my lord into his privy
chamber, making a short supper, or rather a short
repast, and then returned again into the presence
chamber amongst the Frenchmen, behaving himself in so loving a sort and so familiarly towards
them that they could not sufficiently commend him.
And while they were in communication and pas-
time, all their livery were served to their chambers;
every chamber had a basin and ewer of silver, and
a great livery-pot, with plenty of wine and sufficient of every thing."

Such were the merry and gorgeous doings at
Hampton Court, then in all the glory of its newness, in the days of Wolsey's prosperity.   I am
afraid the story of Henry VIII. coming to see this
splendid palace on its first being built, and saying
in a jealous surprise, " My Lord Cardinal, is this a
dwelling for a subject ?" and the courtly Cardinal
replying, " My gracious liege, it is not intended for
a subject ; it is meant only for the greatest and
most bounteous king in Christendom," is too good
to be true ; for although Wolsey did give up this
favourite palace to his royal master, it was long
afterwards, and only on the palpable outbreak of

his displeasure, as a most persuasive peace-offering ; an offering which, though especially acceptable, failed nevertheless to ensure lasting peace. The sun of the great Cardinal was already in its decline. His fair Protestant enemy was in possession of the king's ear and mind, and he had soon to make his sorrowful exclamation :

Farewell ! a long farewell to all my greatness !
This is the state of man : to-day he puts forth
The tender leaves of hope ; to-morrow blossoms,
And bears his blushing honours thick upon him ;
The third day comes a frost, a killing frost ;
And when he thinks, good easy man, full surely
His greatness is a ripening,—nips his root,
And then he falls as I do.   I have ventured,
Like little wanton boys that swim on bladders,
This many summers in a sea of glory ;
But far beyond my depth : my high-blown pride
At length broke under me ; and now has left me,
Weary and old with service, to the mercy
Of a rude stream that must for ever hide me.
Vain pomp and glory of this world, I hate ye !
I feel my heart new opened.   O, how wretched
Is that poor man that hangs on princes' favours !
There is, betwixt that smile we would aspire to,
That sweet aspect of princes and their ruin,
More pangs and fears than wars or women have :
And when he falls, he falls like Lucifer,
Never to rise again !

27*

The story of the ambition and greatness of Wolsey is a splendid and rare story; but what would it have been without his fall? Had he gone down to the grave in the fulness of his age, and the undiminished strength of his power, it would have been looked upon as a wondrous career of prosperity, and would have excited but little curiosity in posterity; but his fall came, to fix it on the heart of all time. Never were mortal fortunes so complete in their light and shade, in their height and depth, as his. While we are gazing on the authority and the gay pageantries of the long life of the great man, as on the brightness of a summer day that seems as if it would shine on for ever; suddenly the clouds blacken overhead, the lightning flames abroad, the tempest falls, with deluging torrents and a rending thunderbolt, and when it is past—we gaze in silent astonishment on a scene of blackened desolation!

The fall of Wolsey is one of the most complete and perfect things in the history of man. The hold which he had so long on that fierce and lionlike king—that passionate and capricious king—is amazing; but at once it gives way, and down he goes for ever. But, great as he was in his prosperity, so is he great in his ruin. There are those who accuse him of servility and meanness, but they do not well comprehend human nature. Wolsey knew himself, his master, and the world; and Shakspeare, whose own heart was the representative of the universal heart of man, has shown that he judged justly of Wolsey's spirit in his delineation of him at this crisis. Wolsey knew himself. He knew his own proud ambition, and he knew that his story must for ever stand a brilliant point in the annals of his country; but to give to it an effect that would cover a multitude of sins, and make him, who had hitherto been a daring adventurer and a despot of no mean degree, an object of lasting commiseration—it was necessary to fall with dignity and die with penitence. He knew his master,—and his favour once gone; his resentment once at the pitch, by the thwarting of his passions; his cupidity once kindled—there was nothing to expect but destruction, certain, and at hand.

> Nay, then, farewell!
> I have touched the highest point of all my greatness;
> And from that full meridian of my glory
> I haste now to my setting: I shall fall
> Like a bright exhalation in the evening,
> And no man see me more.

In the contemplation of Wolsey in his fallen condition, we are so much affected by his humility, his

candour, and his sorrow, that we forget his former
haughtiness and his crimes. He never accuses his
sovereign of injustice; he breaks out in no passion
against him; he acknowledges that he was the creature of his favour, and that all he had—rank and
fortune—were his to take away, as he had given
them. His tears for so great a reverse—for such
a stripping down of power and honour—are natural; and his tears and sorrow for his faithful servants open up the noblest place in his heart, and go
far to make you love and honour him. We cannot
help comparing the cases of Thomas à Becket and
his own; and asking what Wolsey would have done,
had he stood in the situation of that daring and in-
domitable churchman. Probably he might have put
on the same air of menace and defiance. But here
matters were in a different position: Henry VIII.
was not Henry II., nor was the papal power now
of the same terrible force in England. Bluff Harry
was one that could and would have his will, outra-
geous or bloody as it might be; and the spirit of
the Reformation was already shaking the tiara to
the ground in this country. Under these circumstances, a wise and sagacious man would see that
there was nothing for it but to submit,—with sorrow, which must be felt to the core, but with the
decency and grave humility of a fallen statesman;

and, in these respects, the conduct of Wolsey, throughout the melancholy period of his disgrace, must sensibly affect every generous mind. There is nothing in all history more touching and interesting than his progress northward, at the king's command, to retire to his diocese. If any act of his after his fall, can bear the construction of servile or unworthy of him, it was, that when the king's messenger overtook him on his way to Esher, with a ring and a word of comfort from the king, and he alighted from his mule, and, kneeling in the road, kissed the ring and embraced the messenger, sending back his most heartfelt thanks to his highness,—and his jester, as a present that he knew would be especially welcome. But this was in the very moment of his surprise and agony at the king's displeasure, and when he was full of the bruising sense of his unlooked-for fall. Afterwards, as he progressed from Esher to York, his conduct was such as truly seemed to indicate that the words which Shakspeare puts into his mouth—

I feel my heart new opened,

were those of his genuine feeling. How picturesque and solemn that journey! He went, progressing slowly on his way from stage to stage, riding on his mule in a grave sadness, followed by his troop of faithful servants. Wherever he came, people flocked out to see him, and to ask his blessing; and everywhere he administered to their wants. It was then only that he seemed to be the real Christian bishop. Wherever he abode for any length of time—as at Peterborough, Southwell, and Scroby—he became highly popular with both the gentry and the people, and was long after remembered in those places. His train had something still even of his ancient pomp, for it consisted of one hundred and sixty persons, with twelve carts, loaded with goods, and others for the carriage of articles of daily use. He kept the holidays in the most solemn manner, on Palm Sunday going in procession with the monks, and bearing his palm with as much humility as the lowest of the company. On Maunday Thursday he washed and kissed the feet of fifty poor people; gave each twelve pence, three ells of good canvass, for shirts; a pair of shoes; and a cask of red herrings. On Easter-day he went in procession in his cardinal vestments, and sung mass himself solemnly; giving his benediction and "cleane remission to all the hearers." He used all his ability wherever he came to reconcile the differences of the gentry, and to comfort and nourish the poor. Arriving on a wide waste near Ferrybridge, he found upwards of five hundred children assembled round a great stone cross, seeking his blessing and confirmation at his hands. He alighted immediately, and confirmed them all before he would leave the place, so that he did not arrive at Cawood, his destination, until a late hour.

However much of policy there may have been in this conduct of the fallen prelate and prime minister, as we cannot doubt there was considerable, yet it would be more than uncharitable, it would be false to human nature, not to give him credit for feeling deeply the vanity of his past career, and for discovering thus in the last hour, in what the true glory and blessing of humanity really lie. In such a belief, how beautiful and noble are the sentiments which Shakspeare makes him utter, in taking leave of his faithful secretary Cromwell :—

> Let's dry our tears; and thus far hear me, Cromwell!;
> And when I am forgotten, as I shall be,
> And sleep in dull cold marble, where no mention
> Of me more must be heard of,—say I taught thee;
> Say, Wolsey—that once trod the ways of glory,
> And sounded all the depths and shoals of honour,—
> Found thee a way, out of his wreck, to rise in;
> A safe and sure one, though thy master missed it.
> Mark but my fall, and that that ruined me.
> Cromwell, I charge thee, fling away ambition;

By that sin fell the angels; how can man then,
The image of his Maker, hope to win by it?
Love thyself least; cherish those hearts that hate thee:
Corruption wins not more than honesty:
Still in thy right hand carry gentle peace
To silence envious tongues; be just and fear not:
Let all the ends thou aims't at be thy country's,
Thy God's, and truth's; then, if thou fall'st, O Cromwell!
Thou fall'st a blessed martyr.

Lightning Source UK Ltd.
Milton Keynes UK
10 September 2009

143548UK00002B/5/A